I0884527

Sarah Ballenden

Sarah Ballenden

Maureen Hunter

Sarah Ballenden
first published 2017 by
Scirocco Drama
An imprint of J. Gordon Shillingford Publishing Inc.

Scirocco Drama Editor: Glenda MacFarlane
Cover design by Terry Gallagher/Doowah Design Inc.
Author photo by Earl Kennedy
Production photos by Dylan Hewlett
Printed and bound in Canada on 100% post-consumer recycled paper.

We acknowledge the financial support of the Manitoba Arts Council and The Canada Council for the Arts for our publishing program.

Production inquiries to:
Charles Northcote
Core Literary Inc.
140 Wolfrey Avenue
Toronto, Ontario
M4K 1L3
charlesnorthcote7@gmail.com
416-466-4929

Library and Archives Canada Cataloguing in Publication

Hunter, Maureen, 1947-, author
Sarah Ballenden / Maureen Hunter. -- First edition.

A play.
ISBN 978-1-927922-37-8 (softcover)

1. Ballenden, Sarah, 1818?-1853--Drama. I. Title.

PS8565.U5814S27 2017 C812'.54 C2017-905945-9

J. Gordon Shillingford Publishing
P.O. Box 86, RPO Corydon Avenue, Winnipeg, MB Canada R3M 3S3

I dedicate this play

with a heart full of gratitude

to Steven Schipper

Maureen Hunter

Saskatchewan-born, Winnipeg-based Maureen Hunter is one of Canada's most accomplished playwrights. Her work has been produced extensively on Canada's major stages, as well as in Britain and the U.S. and by CBC and BBC Radio. It has been nominated for two Governor General's Literary Awards, two Dora Mavor Moore Awards for Outstanding New Play, and the Lou Siminovitch Prize in Theatre.

Sarah Ballenden, Hunter's latest play, premiered at Royal Manitoba Theatre Centre (RMTC) in Winnipeg in April 2017. Other plays include *Wild Mouth,* premiered by Tarragon Theatre, Toronto, in 2008; *Vinci,* premiered by the National Arts Centre, Ottawa, in co-production with RMTC in 2002; *Atlantis,* premiered in English by RMTC in co-production with Theatre Calgary in 1996 and in French by Théâtre de la Manufacture, Montreal, in 1999; *Transit of Venus,* which premiered at RMTC in 1992 and was given its British premiere by the Royal Shakespeare Company in 1993, its U.S. premiere by the Berkshire Theatre in Stockbridge, Mass., in 1998 and its opera premiere (for which Hunter wrote the libretto) at Manitoba Opera in 2007; and *Footprints on the Moon,* which premiered at Agassiz Theatre, Winnipeg, in 1988 and received its European premiere at the Finborough Theatre in London, England, in 2017.

Hunter's plays have been published individually by Scirocco Drama and Nuage Editions, and in a number of anthologies.

Playwright's Notes and Acknowledgements

Anyone who has delved into the history of the Red River Settlement will have come across the name Sarah Ballenden. Her 1850 trial, parts of which are dramatized here, is one of the most famous in Manitoba legal history. The fact that her name isn't officially attached to the trial—we know it as Foss v. Pelly—is a reflection of the laws of the day, not of her commitment to the proceedings. "I was the first person to get this business investigated," Sarah testified in court. "I had determined to proceed in it."

"This business" was defamation. Sarah's character and reputation were under attack. She was the wife of a Hudson's Bay Company Chief Factor, a position which in fur trade society traditionally commanded respect. One contemporary observed that the wives of Chief Factors, most of whom were "mixed-blood," were treated like queens. Sarah was not. Why? Was it her personality, her behaviour? Did she bring condemnation upon herself? Or were there other forces at work? Was she caught by a shift in equilibrium, a tidal wave of change she couldn't possibly control? These were the questions that drew me to her story.

This play couldn't have been written without access to the rich resources of the Hudson's Bay Company Archives, which for the past twenty-odd years have resided with Manitoba Archives in Winnipeg. There I found not only the transcript of the trial, but a wealth of letters and records that brought Red River to life for me in ways I couldn't have imagined. I'm grateful to those responsible for moving this precious collection from London, England to Winnipeg, and to those who maintain it today. We should all be proud that the HBC collection has been identified by UNESCO as one of the world's most important archives.

I owe a debt of gratitude to Royal Manitoba Theatre Centre, the Winnipeg Arts Council, the Manitoba Arts Council, and the Canada Council for the Arts for financial assistance while I wrote this play. I'm grateful to Dale Gibson, who so generously shared with me his encyclopedic knowledge of the court system of the day, and whose two-volume book, *Law, Life and Government at Red River*, is an historical treasure. Immense gratitude goes to dramaturg Brian Quirt who helped me find my way through the torturous terrain of this story. Most of all, I'm grateful to Steven Schipper for his unflagging encouragement, his faith in my work and his commitment to producing it over nearly thirty years.

All the characters in this play are drawn from historical figures except Flora, who is invented. I have specified the national origins of the characters because I believe that hearing the appropriate accents is essential to understanding the story. Sarah may have spoken a dialect of English with an Orkney lilt called "Bungee," but for the purposes of the play speaks without an accent. So does Flora. Dr. Bunn, because of his education and early influences, speaks with a Scottish accent. Margaret speaks with an acquired English accent.

Historically, the Foss-Pelly trial ran for three days: July 16, 17 and 18, 1850. It was very hot in the Courtroom, so the windows were open. Anyone in Red River who wanted to (which was nearly everyone) could listen to the testimony. The "Bench of two" in the play was, in reality, a Council of seven, including The Major, Thom, and five other fascinating local characters. It has been reduced to two for practical reasons. Members of the Council were allowed to question witnesses.

Under the rules of the Court of the time, plaintiffs and defendants were allowed to make statements to the Court, but could not be questioned. This explains why Mrs. Pelly and Mrs. Davidson, though also defendants, were not called to testify, and why Pelly and Davidson could not legally speak in their own defence.

In the play, the trial opens the play and runs through Scene 12 of Act Two. Scenes outside the Courtroom in Act One occur over a few weeks leading up to the trial. Scenes outside the Courtroom in Act Two occur over a few months following the trial. The final scene occurs in June 1851. In the premiere production, projections were used to assist the audience in understanding where and when each scene occurred. A list of these projections can be found in Appendix I.

A postscript about the major characters appears in Appendix II.

If possible, the following will be present in all the court scenes: Sarah, Foss, Thom, Pelly, Davidson, The Major, and Ballenden after Act One, Scene 11. Miss Anderson, Mrs. Cockran, Margaret and Dr. Bunn are present only when testifying. Simpson, Bishop, and Flora never appear in the Court scenes.

I hear four types of music running through this play: drums, fiddles, bagpipes and a dreary Church organ.

Kohkom is pronounced "coo-come." Clouston is pronounced "clew-stun."

Production History

Sarah Ballenden premiered on the John Hirsch Mainstage at Royal Manitoba Theatre Centre in Winnipeg on April 20, 2017 with the following cast (in alphabetical order):

MAJOR CALDWELL .... John Bluethner

MISS ANDERSON /
BISHOP ANDERSON .... Sarah Constible

JOHN BALLENDEN .... Paul Essiembre

CHRISTOPHER FOSS .... Toby Hughes

AUGUSTUS PELLY .... Tom Keenan

ADAM THOM .... Kevin Klassen

MARGARET BLACK /
FLORA .... Julie Lumsden

SARAH BALLENDEN .... Sera-Lys McArthur

JOHN DAVIDSON /
SIR GEORGE SIMPSON .... Ross McMillan

MRS. COCKRAN /
DR. JOHN BUNN .... Tracey Nepinak

Director .... Steven Schipper

Set and Costume Designer .... Brian Perchaluk

Lighting Designer .... Scott Henderson

Sound Designer .... Michael Wright

Music Composer .... Ted Longbottom

Dramaturg .... Brian Quirt

Title Creation .... Eric Dizon
Fight Director .... Paul Essiembre
Assistant Director .... Erica Wilson
Stage Manager .... Karyn Kumhyr
Assistant Stage Manager .... Kate Duncan
Apprentice Stage Manager .... Zoë Leclerc-Kennedy

Dr. Bunn (Tracey Nepinak) is questioned by Captain Foss (Toby Hughes) before Major Caldwell (John Bluethner) and Adam Thom (Kevin Klassen).

Captain Foss (Toby Hughes), John Ballenden (Paul Essiembre), and Sarah Ballenden (Sera-Lys McArthur) toast their friendship.

Miss Anderson (Sarah Constible) testifies in court before
Major Caldwell (John Bluethner) and Adam Thom (Kevin Klassen).

Sarah Ballenden (Sera-Lys McArthur) comforts John Ballenden
(Paul Essiembre) after he learns a trial is underway.

A court scene. Left to right: John Davidson (Ross McMillan), Augustus Pelly (Tom Keenan), Mrs. Cockran (Tracey Nepinak), Major Caldwell (John Bluethner), Adam Thom (Kevin Klassen), Captain Foss (Toby Hughes), Sarah Ballenden (Sera-Lys McArthur) and John Ballenden (Paul Essiembre).

John Davidson (Ross McMillan) looks on as Augustus Pelly (Tom Keenan) makes a case in their defence before Major Caldwell (John Bluethner), Sarah Ballenden (Sera-Lys McArthur), and Adam Thom (Kevin Klassen).

Margaret Black (Julie Lumsden) listens as Sarah Ballenden (Sera-Lys McArthur) pleads for her support against the slanderers.

John Ballenden (Paul Essiembre) meets his new son, held by Sarah Ballenden (Sera-Lys McArthur).

Setting

Upper Fort Garry, Lower Fort Garry and other locations in the Red River Settlement.

June to December 1850 and June 1851.

Characters

SARAH Ballenden, 32.
Wife of the Chief Factor, Fort Garry. Country-born.

John BALLENDEN, 38.
Her husband. HBC man. A Scot.

Christopher FOSS, 33.
Army man. Irish.

Adam THOM, 48.
Lawyer. HBC man. A Scot.

Augustus PELLY, 31.
Accountant. HBC man. English.

John DAVIDSON, perhaps 50.
Mess cook, Upper Fort. English.

MARGARET Black, 32.
Wife of the Chief Trader, Fort Garry. Country-born.

THE MAJOR, 52.
Governor of Assiniboia. Army man. English.

MISS ANDERSON, 50.
Sister of the Anglican Bishop of Rupert's Land. English.

MRS. COCKRAN, 50.
Anglican Clergy wife. English.

Sir George SIMPSON, 64.
Governor-in-Chief of the HBC. A Scot.

BISHOP Anderson, 52.
First Anglican Bishop of Rupert's Land. English.

DR. John BUNN, 48.
Physician. Country-born.

FLORA, 30.
The Ballendens' maid. Country-born.

Doubling: MRS. COCKRAN / DR. BUNN, MARGARET / FLORA, DAVIDSON / SIMPSON and MISS ANDERSON / BISHOP, for a cast of 10.

Casting Note: SARAH and MARGARET / FLORA must be played by actors of Indigenous descent. MRS. COCKRAN / DR. BUNN could be played by an actor of Indigenous descent.

ACT ONE

Scene 1

A gavel sounds. Lights up on the Courtroom, Red River settlement, July 1850. Day One of the trial. The room is dominated by a massive Hudson's Bay Company crest or Union Jack.

THE MAJOR: Christopher Foss, Esquire versus Augustus Pelly, Esquire and his wife, and John Davidson and his wife! The Plaintiff, Captain Foss, claims that the Defendants have made slanderous public statements accusing him and Mrs. Ballenden of scandalous behaviour. We have convened a special session of the Court to hear this case. We have a jury of twelve and a Bench of two, myself and Mr. Thom. *(Slams the gavel.)* Statement from the Plaintiff, Captain Foss.

FOSS: I wish to assure the Court that I have raised this action not for any pecuniary gain, but to clear the reputation of a lady who has been, as I shall prove, grossly defamed by the Defendants. That lady—*(Gestures to SARAH.)*—is Mrs. Ballenden. I'm asking two hundred pounds in damages from Mr. Pelly and the same from Mr. Davidson.

THE MAJOR: *(Slams the gavel.)* Statement from the Defendants.

PELLY: We object to the constitution of this Court. Don't we, Mr. Davidson? Davidson.

DAVIDSON, who is drunk, hauls himself to his feet.

DAVIDSON: We do, Mr. Pelly.

PELLY: Mr. Thom should not be allowed to sit as a judge in a case in which he has acted as attorney for the Plaintiff.

THE MAJOR: How do you respond to that, Mr. Thom?

THOM: I would have advised the Defendants as well, had they come to me. It's the only fair thing to do, since I'm the only lawyer in the settlement and the Hudson's Bay Company requires that I also serve as a judge.

PELLY: I understand he is also going to testify. Judge, attorney and witness, all in the same trial! How can Mr. Davidson and I possibly believe him to be impartial? How can the jury? How can we defend ourselves when it's all been rigged against us? This isn't a trial, it's a lynching.

THOM: If you were not confident that justice would prevail, you should have kept your mouth shut in the first place.

PELLY: *(Very sharp.)* We demand that our objection be recorded.

THE MAJOR: *(Slams the gavel.)* Record the Defendants' objection.

THOM: Major, for the love of God, where did you get that thing?

THE MAJOR: From a Yankee. They're popular down there.

THOM: Well, put it away, please.

THE MAJOR: Oh, indulge me, Mr. Thom. It makes me think of the Hottentots. I served among them, you know. This is the way they speak: *(Tapping the gavel in time.)* Chick chuck chu chu. Chick chuck chu chu. Isn't it a wonder they understand each other? Chick chuck chu chu. *(Glances around; clears his throat; slams the gavel.)* Instructions to the jury.

THOM: Gentlemen of the jury. Many of you have done your duty, as citizens of Red River, by serving as jurors before. But this is your first experience with defamation.

PELLY: Alleged defamation.

THOM: So I must speak to you about something we call the onus of proof. Although you might assume that Captain Foss must prove that the allegations made against him are untrue, that is not the case. Rather, he must prove that the allegations were made, and that they have damaged his reputation. If he proves those two things to your satisfaction, he need prove nothing else. The Defendants, for their part, can escape liability by proving that their statements were true. But the onus of proof lies with them. Understood? Yes, Mrs. Ballenden.

SARAH: I'd like to be present for the duration of the trial.

THOM: Are you not going to testify?

SARAH: Oh, I'm going to testify.

THOM: Then, strictly speaking, you should not be present when others do.

SARAH: But I was the one who was determined to bring this matter to Court. I'd be serving as Plaintiff myself if the law allowed a married woman to sue on her own behalf. It doesn't, and as my husband was away when I learned about these vicious lies—

PELLY: Lies, are they?

SARAH: Captain Foss volunteered to sue in place of my husband. But it's my trial at the heart of it, my name that has been most tarnished.

PELLY: That's a subjective opinion.

THOM: *(To SARAH.)* You'd be likely to hear many hurtful things.

SARAH: I've heard many hurtful things.

THOM: I suppose we could make an exception, under the circumstances. Major?

THE MAJOR: I never object to the presence of a beautiful woman.

SARAH: I have a second request. I ask the Court, however it rules, to make a clear, definitive statement at the conclusion of this trial as to whether or not the Captain and I have been slandered.

THOM: You want a decisive verdict. Is that what you're saying?

SARAH: After all the talk there's been, I want a verdict that leaves no doubt in anyone's mind as to who is at fault in all this.

FOSS: I wholeheartedly concur.

PELLY: Be careful what you wish for, Captain.

THOM: Mr. Pelly. This is a court of law, not a drawing room. Please keep your asides to yourself.

THE MAJOR: Is it true, Mrs. Ballenden, that all this began because some time ago, you hosted a ladies' tea?

THOM: You need not answer that, Mrs. Ballenden. You are not yet under oath.

SARAH: The answer is yes.

Scene 2

Before the trial. Upper Fort. Chief Factor's Residence. Parlour. SARAH, FOSS and BALLENDEN sit playing cards. In a cradle nearby lies a sleeping baby.

BALLENDEN: *(To SARAH.)* How was the ladies' tea?

SARAH: Dreadful. I disgraced myself. I lost my temper with the Bishop's sister.

BALLENDEN: Sarah.

SARAH: And I shamed the Reverend's wife.

BALLENDEN: Which reverend's wife?

SARAH: Mrs. Cockran.

FOSS: *(Laughs.)* I'd like to have been there for that.

BALLENDEN: Do not encourage her, please. She has too little patience for the clergy.

SARAH: I don't see why there should be more of them in Red River than anywhere else in the British Empire. *(To BALLENDEN.)* I did disgrace myself.

BALLENDEN: Then you must make amends.

SARAH: I will. I'll host a luncheon for all the clergy women, like I did last year. They had a wonderful time, much to their own surprise. It may be an uphill battle with the Bishop's sister here, but even she might unwind a little. Hard as it is to imagine.

FOSS: I understand she's quite strait-laced.

SARAH: Oh, she's a very grand lady. With a very grand nose.

BALLENDEN: Just remember, she's a long way from home. I'm sure she feels as though she's landed at the ends of the earth.

SARAH: My dear Captain Foss, you cannot play that card. I haven't won a hand all evening.

FOSS: My heart goes out to you.

SARAH: You're a devil.

FOSS: So they tell me. *(Gathers up the cards.)*

SARAH: *(To BALLENDEN.)* Look at the grin on his face. He's a man who likes to win.

FOSS: 'Tis usually preferable to losing, I've found. Another game?

SARAH: Another humiliation? No, thank you.

She stands. FOSS stands, then BALLENDEN with some effort.

You're weary, John.

BALLENDEN: Am I?

SARAH: You promised you'd rest for an hour every day. You haven't been doing that.

BALLENDEN: *(To FOSS.)* You see how she torments me. It's a very great burden.

FOSS: I'm sure.

SARAH: *(Caresses his cheek.)* I couldn't bear to lose you, that's why.

FLORA knocks and enters.

FLORA: A courier to see you, Mr. Ballenden. He's waiting in your office.

BALLENDEN: Thank you, Flora. *(To SARAH and FOSS.)* I won't be a moment.

He exits. SARAH moves to the cradle and takes the baby in her arms.

SARAH: Are the children settled, Flora?

FLORA: Catherine says they're all tucked in.

SARAH: Take Baby Frances then, would you? She's fighting it, but she'll sleep now. *(Hands over the baby.)* I'll look in on them a little later. Tell Catherine that, please. And Flora, how is your kohkom?

FLORA: She's a prisoner of her body, she says. All she wants is to die.

SARAH: What a shame. She helped so many people all her life. Who's going to help her now? Is she in pain?

FLORA: She says not. She refuses her own medicine.

SARAH: Let me know if there's anything she needs.

FLORA: Thank you, that's very kind.

FLORA exits with the baby.

FOSS: You look lovely this evening, Mrs. Ballenden.

SARAH: It's Madame Legeault's handiwork. We're lucky to have a seamstress like her in a place the size of this.

FOSS: *(Moves closer.)* Did you really shame the Reverend's wife?

SARAH: I did. I reminded her how her husband—the Reverend Mr. Cockran—once referred to people like me.

FOSS: And how is that?

SARAH: As "the progeny of the adulterer and the whore." That's not a thing you forget. I was ruder still to Miss Anderson—His Honour the Bishop's sister. She means —*(Mimics.)*—"to raise the bar."

FOSS: Does she indeed.

SARAH: She means "to shine the light of Christian goodness into every darkened corner of the settlement. She means to become, if she may be so bold, a model of morality." You can't imagine how superior she is.

FOSS: Oh, I think I can. The English have a knack for that. I know this, being Irish.

SARAH: That's why we get along, you and I. Neither of us quite measures up.

FOSS: Whatever the reason, I'm glad of it.

SARAH: So am I. But I wish your wife and children were here.

FOSS: I'm a career soldier, Mrs. Ballenden. I can't uproot them at every turn.

SARAH: I understand that. But you're planning to make this your home. It would be better all round if you were seen as a family man.

FOSS: Instead of a rogue, you mean?

SARAH: You must miss them very much.

FOSS: I do. Once I've a house to put them in, believe me, I'll send for them. *(Draws a paper from his pocket.)* By the way, since we're having some fun at the clergy's expense, you might enjoy this. It came to me on Sunday after church. *(Reads.)* There once was a bishop so rare/he bought lavender gloves by the pair./ He wore them in church up there on his perch/ 'til the tips of the fingers were bare./ His sermons were lengthy, 'tis true/ but what could the poor fellow do?/ He grew so entranced with his hands as they danced/ he forgot the poor sods in the pews.

SARAH: *(Laughs.)* Well done, Captain, you've caught him precisely. But you mustn't read it to anyone else. Offence will be taken, you know.

SARAH suddenly moves to the sofa and sits.

FOSS: Is something the matter?

SARAH: I've made an enemy of the Bishop's sister.

FOSS: What can she possibly do? You're the leading lady here.

No response.

You'll patch things up at the luncheon.

SARAH: If only my daughters were here. I keep asking John to let them come back, but he insists on a British education. I don't know what they're learning over there.

FOSS: Presumably, to be ladies.

SARAH: So *they'll* think they're superior, too.

FOSS: *(Sits next to her.)* I've never laid eyes on them, of course, but I can tell you this. They'll never hold a candle to their mother.

SARAH: That isn't true.

FOSS: Would I lie to you?

SARAH: It isn't true, but thank you.

They exchange an intimate smile. MRS. COCKRAN enters.

MRS. COCKRAN: Oh my!

She exits.

SARAH: Mrs. Cockran? *(Rises, moves to the door.)* Don't run away. Come and join us.

MRS. COCKRAN re-enters, flustered. FOSS stands.

I wonder where Flora is. You should have been announced.

MRS. COCKRAN: I'm sorry. I was passing, and I thought—

SARAH: I'm glad you came. I owe you an apology for what I said at tea. I shouldn't have quoted your husband. It was very rude of me.

MRS. COCKRAN: *(Wary.)* Why did you?

SARAH: The Bishop's sister got under my skin. But I *am* sorry. I meant to tell you that at the first opportunity. Now come and sit down.

MRS. COCKRAN: *(Not moving.)* Where is Mr. Ballenden?

SARAH: He was called away. But Captain Foss is here.

MRS. COCKRAN: I see that.

FOSS: *(Bows his head.)* Mrs. Cockran.

SARAH: *(To FOSS.)* Mrs. Cockran was my first teacher when I came here to school, all those years ago. *(To MRS. COCKRAN.)* We've known each other forever, haven't we?

MRS. COCKRAN: Almost.

SARAH: Don't stand there. Come and join us.

MRS. COCKRAN: I must go.

SARAH: But you've just arrived.

MRS. COCKRAN: I wanted an apology and now I've got it. Good evening.

MRS. COCKRAN exits.

SARAH: What a strange way to behave.

FOSS: Perhaps she's still upset with you.

SARAH: But I apologized. Twice. I suppose she wanted me down on my knees.

FOSS: She may have misinterpreted our behaviour.

SARAH: Our behaviour? Where's the harm in a smile?

BALLENDEN enters. SARAH turns to him.

You'll never guess what just happened. Mrs. Cockran burst in unannounced and then refused to stay.

BALLENDEN: Just as well. I'm not in the mood for starch right now.

SARAH: But she refused to stay.

BALLENDEN: For pity's sake, Sarah, the woman's allowed to change her mind. Come now. We have not had the luxury of an evening with Captain Foss in a very long time.

SARAH: That's true. We should enjoy it. I'll send for tea.

BALLENDEN: Never mind tea. *(Moves to a table.)* I've a yen for brandy and a good cigar. *(To FOSS.)* What do you say to that?

FOSS: I don't say no.

BALLENDEN: *(Pours drinks.)* Good man.

FOSS: I've been called worse.

BALLENDEN: *(Hands glasses to FOSS and SARAH, raises his own.)* To the Company!

SARAH: Oh, not the Company for once.

BALLENDEN: *(Surprised.)* What, then? The clergy?

SARAH: Toast friendship. There's little enough of that around.

BALLENDEN: To friendship!

FOSS: Friendship! And the beautiful Mrs. Ballenden!

BALLENDEN: Mrs. Ballenden! My beautiful wife.

Scene 3

The Courtroom. Day One of the trial.

THE MAJOR: *(Slams the gavel.)* First witness.

FOSS: Major Caldwell. You *were* subpoenaed, Sir.

THE MAJOR: Yes. A tad irregular, that.

THE MAJOR stands, places his hand on a Bible.

I swear to tell the truth, the whole truth and nothing but the truth, as I would answer to God.

He sits in the witness chair.

FOSS: Please introduce yourself, Sir.

THE MAJOR: Everyone knows me.

FOSS: For the record.

THE MAJOR: William Bletterman Caldwell. I am a soldier and have been so for thirty-five years. I have served three kings; now I serve a queen. I am currently Governor of Assiniboia and commander-in-chief of the British forces here at Red River.

FOSS: Sir. Has Mr. Pelly ever spoken to you about the matter before the Court?

THE MAJOR: He has. He told me that on the night of Mr. Harriott's dinner party—

FOSS: Mr. Harriott being…?

THE MAJOR: Everyone knows—*(Catches himself.)* A former Chief Factor, now retired. Mr. Pelly said that on the night of Mr. Harriott's dinner party, he saw a woman he believed to be Mrs. Ballenden pass from the Chief Factor's residence into your quarters.

SARAH: Outrageous.

FOSS: On what occasion did he tell you this?

THE MAJOR: On the occasion of our discussing Mrs. Ballenden's character.

FOSS: *When* exactly, Sir?

THE MAJOR: Several weeks ago.

FOSS: Was he critical of her character?

THE MAJOR: Critical? I don't know if he was critical or pleased. He told me that she'd once placed her hand on his thigh and given him a look.

FOSS: What kind of look?

THE MAJOR: A significant look, wink wink.

SARAH: On the heads of my children, never.

THOM: You will have your turn to testify, Mrs. Ballenden.

SARAH: Not soon enough.

FOSS: *(To THE MAJOR.)* Sir. Has *Mrs.* Pelly ever spoken to you about the matter before the Court?

THE MAJOR: Several times. She asked me to take a deposition from the German girl of certain facts concerning Mrs. Ballenden.

FOSS: Please clarify for the record who the German girl is.

THE MAJOR: Mrs. Ballenden's personal maid.

PELLY: The one who just left the settlement?

THOM: You're out of order.

PELLY: I'm sorry, I should have said the one who was conveniently sent away.

SARAH: She left of her own accord, on the date that had been planned all along.

THOM: Mrs. Ballenden. I understand how difficult this is for you, but you must stop interrupting the testimony. (*To PELLY.*) As for you, you will have a chance to cross-examine. In the meantime—

PELLY: Fine. But I would ask the Court to bear in mind that Captain Foss has summonsed a great many witnesses in this pathetic excuse for a trial. By the time we get around to ours, we'll have been inundated with one side of the—

THOM: That's enough, Mr. Pelly. Another outburst and I shall have you removed. That would leave Mr. Davidson to present your case. Which could be interesting. *(Loud.)* Are you with us, Mr. Davidson?

DAVIDSON: *(Rouses himself.)* Oh yes, sir. Right as rain.

THOM: Following the testimony, are you?

DAVIDSON: More or less.

THOM: Prepared to present your case, should the need arise?

DAVIDSON: Say what?

THOM: Are you prepared to step into Mr. Pelly's shoes, should I have to have him removed?

DAVIDSON: Oh sir, you mustn't do that.

THOM: Why not?

DAVIDSON: I'm not so good with words, you see. Give me a batch of pickerel or a buffalo shank, I'll cook it up just grand. But words—I don't know why it is. I chase after them.

THOM: You may wish to bear that in mind, Mr. Pelly, and temper your behaviour accordingly.

DAVIDSON: Would you be needing a cook, Mr. Thom? I've lost my job over this. Mrs. Davidson's lost hers, as well. Would you be needing a maid?

PELLY: *(Under his breath.)* Shut up, Davidson.

DAVIDSON: Take the both of us, you've got yourself a bargain.

THOM: No, thank you, Mr. Davidson. Please sit down.

FOSS: Perhaps we should start again. *(To THE MAJOR.)* Mrs. Pelly asked you to take a deposition from the German girl of certain facts concerning Mrs. Ballenden. What were these "certain facts"?

THE MAJOR: That she was too familiar with you. That she went to your rooms at night. That sometimes she placed the German girl to watch, and if Mr. Ballenden should miss his wife, the girl was to say that her mistress had just gone downstairs.

FOSS: Did you take the deposition?

THE MAJOR: No. I told Mrs. Pelly I wanted no part of it. Then she came to me again, saying that the German girl told the scullery maid—

FOSS: Mrs. Davidson?

THE MAJOR: Yes.

FOSS: *(Pointing to DAVIDSON.)* The wife of the Defendant, John Davidson?

THE MAJOR: Yes. The German girl told the scullery maid, who told Mrs. Pelly, that sometimes when Mrs. Ballenden went to your rooms she wore a blanket to disguise herself and at other times the German girl's clothes.

FOSS: Did you agree to take the deposition?

THE MAJOR: No, I refused. It sounded preposterous to me. The girl's about half Mrs. Ballenden's height and twice her width.

FOSS: Was that the end of it?

THE MAJOR: No. She came a third time, saying she'd heard a rumour that Mrs. Ballenden intended to launch a lawsuit. She begged me to take a deposition from the German girl before she left the settlement. I consented, but the girl didn't show.

FOSS: Did Mr. Davidson's wife ever speak to you about the matter before the Court?

THE MAJOR: She came to me a week ago, wanting to make a statement.

DAVIDSON: Wasn't my idea.

THE MAJOR: Something about money Mrs. Ballenden had given her husband to hush him up. By then half the settlement was coming to me for writs and depositions and subpoenas and statements relative to this case. I sent her away.

SARAH: That money was for a cake I'd ordered for the clergy women's luncheon.

THOM: Mrs. Ballenden.

SARAH: I'm sorry, but it's exasperating.

THOM: Further questions, Captain Foss?

FOSS: No, that will be all. Thank you, Major, you've been very helpful.

Scene 4

Before the trial. Upper Fort. Chief Factor's Residence. Bedroom. SARAH sits at a table, going through the mail. BALLENDEN enters.

BALLENDEN: Sarah? What's wrong?

SARAH: The luncheon I was planning for the clergy women. They've all declined.

BALLENDEN: Have they.

SARAH: Every last one. Even Mrs. Cockran.

BALLENDEN: Perhaps the date did not suit.

He sets a carry-all on the bed and begins to lay out his clothes.

SARAH: It's the Bishop's sister. She's behind this.

BALLENDEN: Do not go jumping to conclusions.

SARAH: She doesn't like me.

BALLENDEN: You do not like her.

SARAH: I mean she doesn't *approve*. I knew it the moment we met. I could see the disdain in her eyes.

BALLENDEN: Sarah…

SARAH: John, think about it. You don't decline an invitation to the Chief Factor's residence unless you're on your deathbed.

BALLENDEN: There's probably an explanation.

SARAH: Yes. She's a snob. I'm going to have a word with her.

BALLENDEN: I think you should let it pass.

SARAH: Let it pass?!

BALLENDEN: They'll change their tune soon enough if they find they're not invited to the next Chief Factor's Ball.

SARAH: No, it's far more serious. It's the thin edge of the wedge. There are eight new women in this place—

BALLENDEN: Do I have to hear this again?

SARAH: There are eight English women. If I let the clergy women snub me, they'll all be doing it. The next thing we know they'll be snubbing all the mongrels.

BALLENDEN: I wish you wouldn't use that word.

SARAH: You know what happened before. When Sir George got married and that cad McTavish—

BALLENDEN: Let's not go over that. All this fuss about a silly luncheon.

SARAH: It's not about a silly luncheon. It's about respect. It amazes me that you can't see that.

BALLENDEN: I do not want to quarrel with you. I'm advising you to do what a lady would do, and that is rise above it.

She moves abruptly away. He resumes packing. Beat.

Is there anything you need from me before I go?

SARAH: No.

BALLENDEN: Should anything serious arise, I'd like you to consult Mr. Thom.

No response. He moves to her.

Sweetheart, let's not part like this. I've a journey ahead. It's only Fort Alexander but you never know: I could drown en route.

SARAH: Don't say that.

BALLENDEN: I think you should keep this in perspective. You were rude to the Bishop's sister. There were bound to be repercussions. It will blow over in time. Will you keep it in perspective?

SARAH: *(Against her will.)* I'll try.

He goes back to packing. She moves next to him to help.

Are you looking forward to seeing Sir George?

BALLENDEN: Aye. Like an aching tooth.

SARAH: How long this time?

BALLENDEN: As long as it takes him to convince us he's right about everything. Six weeks, perhaps. He intends to spend a few months afterwards at the Lower Fort. He asked me to have the Big House prepared.

SARAH: Pomp and circumstance. I hope he behaves himself while he's there.

BALLENDEN: What do you mean?

SARAH: I hope he doesn't decide he needs *a bit of brown*.

BALLENDEN: Sarah!

SARAH: Well.

BALLENDEN: He's a changed man since he took a bride.

SARAH: Hmm.

BALLENDEN: You do not believe me. You're perhaps too hard on him.

SARAH: I know what he is, that's all. I know how many women he's bedded and impregnated, then cast off when he tired of them.

BALLENDEN: He did find husbands for some of them.

SARAH: He bought them husbands, you mean.

BALLENDEN: *(Deep sigh.)* Ah, Sarah, you tire me at times.

SARAH: Do I? (*Embraces him.*) The last thing in the world I want is to be tiresome to you.

BALLENDEN: I know, sweetheart. I know.

An intimate moment.

SARAH: You'll think about what I asked you.

BALLENDEN: I would hate to compromise their education.

SARAH: Pooh. Another dance step, another piece of embroidery.

BALLENDEN: French, Latin, the classics. Piano and harp. Deportment.

SARAH: That's what I mean. I hardly recognize them anymore, the things they write about. They're going to forget me, John, like I've forgotten my mother. I remember so little about her. I remember warmth and tenderness. I remember being hugged. I know she sang to me, but in her own tongue so I can't remember the songs. I can't even remember her voice. I don't want that for my girls. It's not enough.

BALLENDEN: I'll think about it, Sarah.

SARAH: And if you won't bring them back, ask Sir George about furlough. You must be as anxious to see them as I am.

BALLENDEN: I'll think about that, too. Any further instructions, Mrs. Ballenden?

SARAH: I'd like you to say goodbye to Catherine.

BALLENDEN: The German girl? I'll be glad to see the back of her. Sly little thing.

SARAH: She's been wonderful with the children.

BALLENDEN: Say goodbye on my behalf.

SARAH: John. After two years.

BALLENDEN: All right, all right.

He snaps his bag closed. Children are heard laughing, off-stage.

SARAH: You'll see the children before you go?

BALLENDEN: Of course.

SARAH: Promise me you'll take care of yourself. You've seemed so much stronger of late.

BALLENDEN: I have been much stronger, thank God. What will you do in my absence?

SARAH: Pine. *(Kisses him.)* Give my regards to Sir George. The pawky little rooster.

BALLENDEN: Pawky. I have not heard that word since I was a child.

SARAH: It's the Scot in me. It surfaces, once in a while.

Scene 5

The Courtroom. Day One of the trial. THE MAJOR as witness.

THOM: You may cross-examine, Mr. Pelly.

PELLY: Major. You told the Court that at Mrs. Pelly's request, you agreed to take a deposition from the German girl, but the girl didn't show. Where was she?

THE MAJOR: Locked up, apparently.

PELLY: By whom?

THE MAJOR: You should know. You're the one who told me.

PELLY: Who do you think locked her up?

THOM: *(To PELLY.)* You're leading the witness.

PELLY: Would it be fair to say that based on the reasons Mrs. Pelly gave you for wanting the German girl's deposition, had it been taken it would have been damaging to Mrs. Ballenden?

THE MAJOR: If that's what the German girl had deposed, it certainly would have.

PELLY: In other words, if anyone in Red River had a reason to prevent the German girl from deposing, it was Mrs. Ballenden.

SARAH: For the love of God, we have her deposition.

PELLY: Oh yes, you'd have insisted on that.

SARAH: It was given freely.

PELLY: It was bought.

THOM: Enough! Move on, Mr. Pelly.

PELLY: I only ask the Court to ponder whether a servant girl might make a very different statement to a figure of imperial authority like the Major than she would to her own mistress, to whom she felt indebted.

THOM: *(Fiercely.)* Move on.

PELLY: Major. You've had your differences with Captain Foss, have you not?

THE MAJOR: I have indeed. The first time was on the ship coming over. I had to deal with an accusation that the Captain had cheated at cards.

FOSS: Be fair, Sir. Who accused me?

THE MAJOR: Mr. Pelly.

PELLY: For good reason. Twenty pounds he cheated me of.

FOSS: *(To PELLY.)* Sure, if I had to cheat to beat a loser like you, I'd give up cards forever.

THOM: Order, please.

PELLY: (*To THE MAJOR.)* Is it true that not long after your arrival in Red River, you suspended Captain Foss as second-in-command?

THE MAJOR: I did.

PELLY: You later reinstated him. Why?

THE MAJOR: I had no one to replace him with. Besides, I was prevailed upon by the Ballendens. They missed his company at mess.

THOM: The point of this, Mr. Pelly?

PELLY: In your own words, Mr. Thom, Captain Foss has to prove that the allegations he claims have been made against him have damaged his reputation. To which I reply: what reputation? Even his commanding officer lacks confidence in him.

FOSS: 'Tis you on trial, Pelly, not me.

PELLY: Perhaps I should reword that. Perhaps the Captain does have a reputation—as a gambler, an insubordinate, a hot-headed Irish cheat who might still be suspended from his duties if it weren't for the intervention of the Ballendens. Thank you, Major, that will be all.

THOM: Questions, Mr. Davidson? Davidson, for the love of God, take a seat and keep it before you injure yourself. Would you like a glass of water?

DAVIDSON: *(Sits.)* No, sir, I'm not that desperate.

Scene 6

Before the trial. Upper Fort. Chief Factor's Residence. Parlour. SARAH paces. FOSS enters.

FOSS: The boy said urgent.

SARAH: It is. A terrible thing has happened. There are lies being spread about us, the worst kind of lies. They're even saying—they're saying—that Baby Frances is not John's child.

FOSS: Not Mr. Ballenden's? Mine?!

SARAH: Thank God he isn't here.

FOSS: But—who's spreading this filth?

SARAH: Davidson, for one.

FOSS: Your mess cook? The man's a drunk. Who'd credit him?

SARAH: And his wife, the scullery maid.

FOSS: The skullduggery maid, you mean. Worst gossip in the settlement.

SARAH: The Pellys have been at it too.

FOSS: The Pellys?

SARAH: Imagine. My husband's accountant and—that wife of his.

FOSS: The scoundrel. The snivelling—

FOSS wheels around and starts off.

SARAH: Where are you going?

FOSS: To shoot the man.

SARAH: Stop.

FOSS: To thrash him, then.

SARAH: Control yourself.

FOSS: I'll have a swipe at his wife, while I'm at it. The simpering thing.

SARAH: Captain.

FOSS: I know, I know, I must calm myself. I *will* calm myself.

SARAH: I'll pour you a brandy. *(Moves to do so.)* I'm still in shock myself.

FOSS: Who told you?

SARAH: Catherine, my maid.

FOSS: The German girl?

SARAH: She's going back to Sault Ste Marie. I gave her a gift I'd promised her, and the whole business came pouring out. (*Hands him a brandy.)* It seems they've been going at it behind our backs for some time.

FOSS: You're sure Mr. Ballenden doesn't know?

SARAH: He didn't when he left.

FOSS: He'll never quite trust me again.

SARAH: Why do you say that?

FOSS: I know how men think.

SARAH: We have to fight it, then.

FOSS: It might be wiser not to. Servants gossip, they always have. 'Tis usually best to ignore it.

SARAH: Maybe I could if it was just the servants. The Pellys are another thing.

FOSS: I can see why he'd go after me. He likes to gamble and he's lousy at it. I've been obliged to take his money, more often than he'd like. What they have against *you* I can't imagine. *(Beat.)* Unless you spurned him. You did, didn't you.

SARAH: How did you know that? Even John doesn't know.

FOSS: 'Tis written all over him.

SARAH: It was before he was married. I hoped once he had a wife of his own—

FOSS: No luck there. He only took her to please his father. He confessed as much at cards. No doubt she knows it, too. And she probably knows how he feels about you. I really should shoot the bastard. Excuse my language, Mrs. Ballenden, but by God, you don't deserve this.

SARAH: Neither do you.

FOSS: (*Laughs.*) An Irishman in an English army? A man with an eye for an easy gain?

SARAH: Don't demean yourself, please.

FOSS: I'm an opportunist. I've never said otherwise. If the Company hadn't offered land, I wouldn't be here now. 'Tis the land I came for. Another four years and 'tis mine free and clear. Then I'll be set. For you, of course, 'tis different. What are we going to do?

SARAH: Confront the Pellys in person.

FOSS: They'd expect us to deny it. That wouldn't change a thing. We could meet with the clergy wives, I suppose. Set the record straight.

SARAH: Go crawling to them? I couldn't. My husband is Chief Factor. It's they who should come to me.

FOSS: Then perhaps we should let it go.

SARAH: I won't be lied about. I won't have Mr. Ballenden wondering even for a second whether the lies are true. I won't have my children hearing stories about me. I won't be remembered for a scandal that never happened. We should see Mr. Thom.

FOSS: Mr. Thom? Better not to involve the law. In a place like this, it gets muddy. Nothing but amateurs.

SARAH: Mr. Thom's not an amateur. He'd be a great asset to us.

FOSS: I don't think we want this to get out of hand.

SARAH: I don't see why it should.

FOSS: You don't know lawyers, then.

SARAH: We can at least hear what he has to say.

FOSS: I suppose.

SARAH: Besides, it's what John would want. *(Beat.)* I've never seen you look so grim.

FOSS: I have a strange presentiment that I'm about to be cast as knight in shining armour. 'Tis not a role that suits me.

SARAH: You might surprise yourself.

FOSS: I might. Would there be anything in it for me, do you think?

SARAH: *(Laughs.)* You always have to play the rogue, don't you, Captain Foss?

FOSS: Apparently, Mrs. Ballenden.

SARAH: We'll give the Pellys a run for their money. The Bishop's sister, too.

Scene 7

The Courtroom. Day One of the trial. MISS ANDERSON as witness. THE MAJOR is back on the Bench.

MISS ANDERSON: *(To THOM, indicating FOSS.)* Must I be questioned by this man?

THOM: What is your objection?

MISS ANDERSON: My brother the Bishop, if he were here, would be aghast that a lady of my stature was to be imposed upon by such a man.

FOSS: By an Irishman, do you mean?

MISS ANDERSON: *(To THOM.)* By a man whom the Bishop does not consider a gentleman.

FOSS: He said that?

MISS ANDERSON: Am I to answer his questions, Mr. Thom?

FOSS: Did he say why he had formed that opinion?

MISS ANDERSON: Mr. Thom!

THOM: *(To FOSS.)* You'd better let me put the questions. May I have your notes?

FOSS hands THOM his notes. THOM turns to MISS ANDERSON.

How long have you known Mrs. Pelly?

MISS ANDERSON: We came over on the same ship together, though she was Miss Clouston then. My brother married her to Mr. Pelly on our arrival at York Factory. The first marriage performed in Rupert's Land by the very first bishop!

THOM: Bishop Provencher across the river might well take issue with that.

MISS ANDERSON: I mean the first *real* bishop.

THOM is momentarily taken aback.

THOM: How would you describe your relationship with Mrs. Pelly?

MISS ANDERSON: We're very good friends.

THOM: Has she spoken to you about the matter before the Court?

MISS ANDERSON: *(Evasively.)* What matter, exactly?

THOM: Has she told you that she believed Mrs. Ballenden and Captain Foss were engaged in a relationship?

MISS ANDERSON: What kind of relationship?

FOSS: For the love of—

THOM: An adulterous one. Miss Anderson?

MISS ANDERSON: My brother the Bishop will be ever so upset when he returns from his travels to find I've been interrogated like this. In front of all these men. On such a subject. I've never been married, you know.

THOM: *(Forcefully.)* Has Mrs. Pelly ever told you she believed that Mrs. Ballenden and Captain Foss were engaged in an adulterous relationship?

MISS ANDERSON: *(With righteous fury.)* Only as something to be deeply regretted! *(Collects herself.)* Excuse me. I don't mean to lose my temper. It's just that I so seldom sleep. The wolves, you see, howling. It's enough to drive one mad. And if I never hear another drum beat, or fiddle screech, or bagpipe wail, I'll know I've gone to heaven. You may proceed.

THOM: You were recently invited by Mrs. Ballenden to a luncheon at the Chief Factor's residence, were you not?

MISS ANDERSON: I was.

THOM: You declined the invitation. Why?

MISS ANDERSON: Mrs. Pelly and I discussed the invitation and we agreed it would be inappropriate for me to attend.

THOM: Why inappropriate?

MISS ANDERSON: Because of Mrs. Ballenden's reputation.

THOM: Which Mrs. Pelly had enlightened you upon.

MISS ANDERSON: I have a mind of my own, you know. I have eyes and ears.

THOM: Meaning?

MISS ANDERSON: Mrs. Ballenden had me to tea soon after I arrived. I didn't feel her home was run to the proper standard. One of her servants was eavesdropping. That would never happen at the Bishop's residence, let me assure you of that. And it was apparent that Mrs. Ballenden has an unfortunate attitude.

THOM: Please explain.

MISS ANDERSON: I accompanied my brother to Red River not only to run his household, but to serve as an example to the population here of English mor—*(Catches herself.)*—sensibilities. When I attempted to explain that to Mrs. Ballenden, she took offence.

THOM: In fact, did you not say that you intended to *raise the bar?* To be *a model of morality?*

MISS ANDERSON: I may have used those words.

THOM: As though there was no one here to set a moral standard.

MISS ANDERSON: There are ladies here, but only a handful.

THOM: Are you suggesting that you do not consider Mrs. Ballenden a lady?

MISS ANDERSON: Well, she was born here, wasn't she?

SARAH: *(To MISS ANDERSON.)* All the men on the jury were either born here or are married to women who were. You're saying that the mothers and wives of these men are by definition less than ladies.

MISS ANDERSON: Well, I'm—

SARAH: That attitude is not welcome in Red River, no matter whose sister you are. It's not welcome and we won't have it.

THE MAJOR: Order!

SARAH: Our roots go down forever in this country.

THE MAJOR: Mrs. Ballenden!

SARAH: You can't come here and treat us like this.

THE MAJOR: *(Slams the gavel.)* Order!

SARAH: We won't stand for it!

Scene 8

Before the trial. Red River Settlement. THOM'S office. SARAH, FOSS and THOM.

THOM: Has it occurred to you that you could lose?

SARAH: We won't lose.

THOM: May I play the devil's advocate?

SARAH: Of course.

THOM: What is the nature of your relationship with one another?

FOSS: What do you mean?

THOM: It has not escaped my notice—and will not have escaped the notice of others—that you enjoy one another's company.

SARAH: We do.

FOSS: That's no crime, surely.

THOM: You like to flirt, Captain Foss. *(To SARAH.)* You're quite a good flirt yourself. Is it possible you've been careless?

SARAH: The Captain is a perfect gentleman. He's been a friend to both of us—Mr. Ballenden and me.

THOM: A lot of eyes are on you. A friendship between the two of you, even an innocent one, is bound to be suspect in certain quarters.

SARAH: If Mr. Ballenden has no objection to our friendship, neither should anyone else.

THOM: All right. But you do not necessarily have to sue. There are other options.

SARAH: Such as?

THOM: You could simply let it blow over.

SARAH: That's out of the question.

FOSS: 'Tis.

THOM: You could undertake a private investigation. It would be much more discreet than a trial.

SARAH: More whispering behind closed doors. I don't see the point in that.

FOSS: Nor do I. It must be out in the open, so the liars are seen for what they are.

THOM: At least wait until Mr. Ballenden returns. How long will it be? A few weeks.

SARAH: I have something to tell you in confidence. Sir George intends to transfer Mr. Pelly to Fort Vancouver. He and his wife will be leaving here as soon as my husband returns. If I don't move quickly, they'll be gone, and the slander will spread to Vancouver.

THOM: If you sue them, Mrs. Ballenden, the slander will be all through the Company.

SARAH: But by then we'll have proved them wrong.

THOM: I wish I shared your confidence. If only Mr. Ballenden were here! I'd rather he made the decision.

SARAH: Well, as to that, my husband, the best of all men—*(Breaks off.)* He's very fragile just now.

THOM: I rather thought he'd recovered.

SARAH: He pretends he has, but he's not the man he was before he had his stroke. He frets, he wrestles with decisions. I don't want him to have to wrestle with this. I want to lay this business to rest before he comes back.

THOM: That's optimistic, I'm afraid. Even if I called a special session of the Court, it's unlikely it could sit on such short notice.

SARAH: We could at least have it underway—the process underway—to spare him the decision.

THOM: *(Beat.)* We could.

SARAH: And you'll represent us, Mr. Thom.

THOM: I would do it gladly, as I would gladly assist your husband in anything he asked. But I cannot represent you.

SARAH: Why not?

THOM: Because if you go to court, I'll have to sit on the bench.

FOSS: I'll do it, then. I'll represent the both of us.

THOM: *(To FOSS.)* Do you think you can plead the case?

FOSS: I'll do my very best.

THOM: I'll advise you, if you wish. I've had to do that before in this place. I've even had to advise both sides, and then preside as judge. That's Red River for you. *(To SARAH.)* Will you testify?

SARAH: In a heartbeat.

THOM: Good. *(To FOSS.)* You'll want to be certain that when she does, it falls at just the right time. Not a moment too soon, not a moment too late. You'll want to line up your witnesses. The sooner you summons them, the better.

Scene 9

Before the trial. Upper Fort. Chief Factor's Residence. Parlour. SARAH and MARGARET.

MARGARET: What do you mean, I may be summonsed?

SARAH: You may have to testify in court. On behalf of the Plaintiff, Captain Foss. Which is to say, me. If you've heard the gossip about us, and you have.

MARGARET: Why do you say that?

SARAH: The other day after church, you lowered your head when you saw me and scurried away.

MARGARET: I'm embarrassed you're suing the Pellys. It doesn't reflect well on the Company.

SARAH: That sounds like your husband speaking.

MARGARET: He is Chief Trader, after all. He's entitled to an opinion.

SARAH: Margaret, you've heard the gossip. Why didn't you tell me? You're my oldest friend in the world.

MARGARET: My husband asked me not to.

SARAH: Oh, Margaret, how you've changed. If that's what an English education does… Or marriage to Mr. Black.

MARGARET: He wants me to be accepted.

SARAH: You are.

MARGARET: By ladies.

SARAH: *(Turns to her.)* That's why I've seen so little of you.

MARGARET: *(Uncomfortably.)* We're at the Lower Fort now, as you know very well. I can't just walk across the yard and call on you.

SARAH: Margaret, tell me the truth. Do *you* think they're better than me?

MARGARET: Sarah, can't you see? It's not that I think they're better than you, it's that *they* think they are. They think they're better than me, as well, but I've been—educated—

SARAH: In England, yes.

MARGARET: I've learned how to deal with them.

SARAH moves away.

Sarah?

SARAH: I was seven when I came to Red River. The last thing I wanted to do. "You must learn to be a lady," my father said. "You won't learn that in the Athabasca country." So I left the forests and the great river valleys, and I crossed half the continent in the care of my guardian to come to school here. I learned what it was to be homesick, to be ill with longing for home. I cried myself to sleep at night. I missed my parents, my brothers and sisters. *(Turns to her.)* You had the cot next to mine. We came to be such good friends. When one of the teachers called you a lazy half-breed, I took the yardstick to her. I took the beating after. You'd have done the same for me. We laughed a lot. We shed some tears. Then you went off to England.

MARGARET: That's not fair. I've spoken well of you, often.

SARAH: In your acquired English accent.

MARGARET: Your own daughters are over there now, acquiring the same bloody accent.

SARAH: Listen to me. When John was appointed Chief Factor and we came back to Red River, we were welcomed with open arms by the Company men and their wives. Of course, John has always been popular, but it wasn't only him. Old Mr. Ross told me—forgive me for repeating this—that I was in a position to raise all the country-borns above the English ladies here, and that I was sure to do it. And now look at this. And all because of a few women, a few intolerant snobs.

MARGARET: It's a little more complicated than that.

SARAH: You weren't here when it happened before. When Sir George married his cousin—his *tender flower*—and brought her out from England. And suddenly the word went out: country-born women were not welcome at the Lower Fort. I was just a girl but I remember the shock that ran through the place. Even your mother, Margaret, was not welcome there. She must have told you about it.

MARGARET: Yes. She was very hurt.

SARAH: It was a terrible time. In that same year that cad McTavish turned off Nancy. Seventeen years, seven children, and he came back from furlough with a Scottish bride on his arm.

MARGARET: We have the Church to protect us now.

SARAH: No one will protect us if we don't stand up to them. All of us mongrels, together. We can do it if we support one another. There are far more of us than there are of them.

MARGARET: Not for long.

SARAH: We owe it to our mothers, our grandmothers.

MARGARET: What about our daughters?

SARAH: Even more.

MARGARET: *(Quietly.)* I don't agree.

SARAH: Margaret, say what you mean.

MARGARET: You want me to stand beside you now. Why should I? You've brought this on yourself by the way you behave. You've been reckless. I would never risk compromising my reputation as you have done. Our behaviour has to be beyond reproach, always, or the knives come out. I told you that. I warned you. And besides, I've seen the future, and I want to be part of it. I want that for my children, too.

SARAH: Yes, you've made that very clear. Good day, Mrs. Black.

MARGARET: Don't be like that.

SARAH: Get out.

MARGARET starts off, but turns back.

MARGARET: If you summons me, you'll be sorry.

SARAH: What's that supposed to mean?

MARGARET: Good day, Mrs. Ballenden.

MARGARET exits.

SARAH: Just for that, I'll do it.

Scene 10

After Day One of the trial. Lower Fort. A Company office. SIMPSON paces. BALLENDEN enters.

BALLENDEN: Sir George. I was just going on to the Upper Fort. Has something come up?

SIMPSON: *(Brandishes a document.)* What do you suppose I have here? A sworn statement from your accountant, Augustus Pelly, and your mess cook, John Davidson, asserting their personal knowledge that your wife has been engaged in an adulterous relationship with Captain Christopher Foss.

BALLENDEN staggers. SIMPSON throws down the document and picks up another.

What do you suppose this is? A letter from Bishop Anderson advising me that one of my officers, Augustus Pelly, has been charged with slander. By Captain Foss, on behalf of your wife. There's a public trial underway, for God's sake.

BALLENDEN: A trial?

SIMPSON: Half of Red River will be on the stand. You'd better sit down, Ballenden, you're as white as a sheet.

BALLENDEN sinks into a chair.

I want you to know that this is the most deplorable situation any of my officers has gotten himself into, and believe me, that's saying something. Your name will be dragged through the mud. That's bad enough, but the name of the Hudson's Bay Company will be dragged along with it, and that is intolerable. And all because you, Ballenden, have failed to control your wife.

BALLENDEN: I have to say, I'm—flabbergasted.

SIMPSON: I warned you, you may recall, when you decided to marry her. I suggested that a man of your ability and with your prospects would be wise not to choose a country-born girl, but that if you did, you would need a firm hand.

BALLENDEN: I do not understand. Captain Foss is a particular friend—

SIMPSON: And that's another thing. A gentleman is judged by the company he keeps. Foss is pleasant enough, I suppose, but I question his character. The Major has never been high on him. I'm disappointed in you, Ballenden. I expected better.

BALLENDEN: *(Hesitates.)* Are you asking for my resignation as Chief Factor?

SIMPSON: I would not refuse it, if you were to tender it, provided you assured me you'd devote the time to sorting out your personal life. You'd still be a Company officer, of course. We'd call it furlough.

BALLENDEN: In that case, I resign.

THOM enters.

SIMPSON: Mr. Thom! Since when do you come barging in?

THOM: I'm sorry, but Mrs. Ballenden was most anxious that I be the first to speak to her husband.

SIMPSON: If it's about her adultery, he knows.

THOM: Why, Sir George, you seem to forget that if there's such a thing as adultery, there's such a thing as perjury.

SIMPSON: You're not involved in this, I hope. I'd be very disappointed if you were.

THOM: It's too late, Sir George. It's far too late. *(To BALLENDEN.)* I've brought Dr. Bunn, and a carriage. We'll drive you on to the Upper Fort.

THOM helps BALLENDEN to his feet.

SIMPSON: Mr. Thom. I'm advising you to disengage yourself.

THOM: I heard you, Sir George.

THOM and BALLENDEN exit.

SIMPSON: Consider yourself warned!

Scene 11

Later the same day. Upper Fort. Chief Factor's Residence. Parlour. SARAH, BALLENDEN and FOSS.

BALLENDEN: How many witnesses?

FOSS: Twenty-one. And Pelly has a dozen.

BALLENDEN: My God, we'll be at it forever.

FOSS: I wanted to be on the safe side.

BALLENDEN: Of course. I do not mean to criticize, it's just so—

SARAH: Monstrous.

FOSS: Unexpected.

BALLENDEN: Aye.

FOSS: It will take about three days, we think. The first day went well, overall. The Major was strong. He'd heard the slander from all of them but Davidson. In fact, I've had a hard time finding anyone who can implicate Davidson.

SARAH: Except Catherine.

BALLENDEN: Your maid? But she's gone, is she not?

SARAH: We have her statement.

FOSS: It's a good one. I'm debating whether to have it read before Mrs. Ballenden testifies, or afterwards. There are advantages either way. I may have to just play it by ear.

SARAH: You see what good hands we're in, John.

FOSS: Please. Don't say that yet.

BALLENDEN: I'm very grateful, Captain.

FOSS: 'Tis Mr. Thom you should thank. He's been an enormous help.

BALLENDEN: I hope that does not come back on him. Sir George was not pleased to learn he was involved.

FOSS: Will he attend the rest of the trial?

BALLENDEN: No. He'll hunker down at the Lower Fort, and fume. I've never seen him so furious.

SARAH: He'll fire Pelly, I hope.

BALLENDEN: I doubt it. Pelly's too well connected. But it would not take me more than five minutes to have the bastard transferred.

SARAH: But you said he—

BALLENDEN: I said he was going to Vancouver. He's not, after all. He changes his mind, Sir George, like others change their socks.

SARAH: They have to be gone from this place. I can't bear to look at the man.

BALLENDEN: How will you handle his questioning, then?

SARAH: I'll handle it.

FOSS: The whole settlement is on edge, waiting for her testimony. It's all they talk about, I'm told. Well, that about covers it. We'll start off tomorrow with Dr. Bunn. He'll be strong, I'm sure.

FLORA enters, distraught.

SARAH: What is it, Flora?

FLORA: I'm sorry to interrupt, Mrs. Ballenden — Mr. Ballenden, Captain — but — *(To SARAH.)* — my grandmother is begging to see you.

SARAH: How is she?

FLORA: Very low. She keeps asking for you. I told her the timing couldn't be worse, but she keeps insisting.

SARAH: Does she need any Company medicine?

FLORA: No, Mrs. Ballenden. She needs you.

SARAH: Fetch a shawl and my walking boots. We'll go straight there.

FLORA exits. SARAH moves to BALLENDEN.

I'm sorry. Her grandmother is dying. I can't refuse. I'll be back as soon as I can. The children will be thrilled to see you.

SARAH exits. Beat.

FOSS: I hope you feel I've done the right thing. I felt certain you wouldn't want me to stand idly by, under the circumstances.

BALLENDEN: Of course not. As I said, I'm grateful. It's a dirty business, though.

FOSS: 'Tis.

BALLENDEN: It's a very dirty business.

Scene 12

The Courtroom. Day Two of the trial. BUNN as witness. BALLENDEN is now present.

FOSS: Please tell the Court who you are.

DR. BUNN: Dr. John Bunn. I'm a family physician, Coronor of Assiniboia and a proud son of the country. I was born at York Factory and educated in Edinburgh, but I choose to live and work here.

FOSS: Has Mr. Pelly ever told you that he intended to ruin my reputation?

DR. BUNN: He has.

PELLY: I believe I said it would be easy to do, since it was already in such disrepair.

FOSS: Did Mr. Pelly say *why* he wished to ruin my reputation?

DR. BUNN: He said that you cheated at cards and that your behaviour towards Mrs. Ballenden was improper.

FOSS: How did you respond to that?

DR. BUNN: I told him that I'd often played cards with you and while I'd rarely known you to lose, I'd never known you to cheat. As to the second complaint, I told him he would be well-advised to pay less attention to Mr. Ballenden's wife and more to his own.

FOSS: Have you been in the company of the Ballendens when I was present?

DR. BUNN: Often, at their home and at mess.

FOSS: Have you ever witnessed improper behaviour between Mrs. Ballenden and me?

DR. BUNN: Never.

FOSS: Have you ever witnessed anything in Mrs. Ballenden's behaviour that would suggest she was unhappy in her marriage?

DR. BUNN: I have never seen Mrs. Ballenden treat her husband with anything but the greatest kindness. She has always been deeply concerned about his health and well-being. It is perhaps her foremost concern, after the children.

FOSS: The Major has testified that Mr. Pelly told him that on the night of Mr. Harriott's dinner party, he saw a woman he believed to be Mrs. Ballenden cross into my quarters. Did you attend Mr. Harriott's dinner party?

DR. BUNN: I did, though I left rather early, as you and I had a date for cards.

FOSS: In my quarters?

DR. BUNN: In your quarters.

FOSS: Do you think it possible that I could have had a rendezvous with a woman while I was playing cards with you?

DR. BUNN: You'd have been a very busy man.

FOSS: Thank you, Dr. Bunn.

PELLY: Dr. Bunn. Has Mr. Ballenden ever indicated to you that his marriage was unhappy?

DR. BUNN hesitates.

Would you like me to repeat the question?

DR. BUNN: No. *(After a moment.)* I rode up from the Lower Fort with Mr. Ballenden last evening, just after he learned that the Defendants had accused his wife of adultery. He was, as one would expect, extremely distressed.

He confessed to me that during her last pregnancy, his wife had proposed that they separate.

SARAH: *(To BALLENDEN, deeply shocked.)* John!

PELLY: Thank you, Dr. Bunn.

Scene 13

After Day Two of the trial. Upper Fort. Chief Factor's Residence. Bedroom. SARAH and BALLENDEN.

BALLENDEN: I never dreamed he'd repeat that. I was staggered at the time. Wracking my brain for any reason you might actually—

SARAH: John.

BALLENDEN: Well.

SARAH: Now the whole settlement knows.

BALLENDEN: The settlement? It will be all through the Company by the end of the year. *(Glances at her.)* I'm sorry, sweetheart. I can see you've been crying.

SARAH: Not about that.

BALLENDEN: What, then?

SARAH: When I saw Flora's grandmother last night—*(Breaks off, upset.)*

BALLENDEN: What happened?

SARAH: I never knew my grandmothers, either of them. I barely knew my mother. Wasn't with her when she died. I walked into that room last night completely unprepared. It was quite a shock. Do you know why she wanted to see me? To give me her courage. She won't be needing it any more, she said, but she fears I will. And now I feel such unease. I can't begin to describe it. Maybe this was all a mistake.

BALLENDEN: A little late for that. *(Turns away.)* It's the strain of the trial. Having to sit there, hour after hour, while our intimate lives are laid bare. It's almost too much to endure.

SARAH: But we will endure it.

BALLENDEN: I only hope I get my job back.

SARAH: Get it back? What are you talking about?

BALLENDEN: I tendered my resignation to Sir George. But I'm sure he'll let me withdraw it. He'd have to appoint Mr. Black in my place, and I know he's not keen on him.

SARAH: You resigned your position before you'd even heard my side. You might as well have pronounced me guilty!

BALLENDEN: Imagine what it's like! To stand before Sir George Simpson, Governor of the Hudson's Bay Company, while two of your own employees—

SARAH: Declare your wife a whore.

BALLENDEN: They had *personal knowledge.*

SARAH: Your wife of fourteen years who's never deceived you.

BALLENDEN: Perhaps if it had not been Captain Foss.

SARAH: What's that supposed to mean?

BALLENDEN: I know how fond you are of him.

SARAH: You're fond of him, too.

BALLENDEN: I am, of course I am. But sometimes the way he looks at you... And after all, he's alone. He's been alone a good while now. Had it been any other man—

SARAH: No, there's no excuse. There's no excusing this, John. I've loved you faithfully. Nursed you, borne your children. Let you send them away. Tried to please you with every breath. But you trusted them over me. Pelly and Davidson. How could you?

BALLENDEN: Sir George got on his high horse. In fact, he rather insisted.

SARAH: And you couldn't stand up to him. Not even for me. You're no better than that cad McTavish.

BALLENDEN: McTavish? You'll not compare me to him.

SARAH: Who to, then, your father? Next you'll be abandoning me. Finding yourself a respectable wife.

BALLENDEN: I will not listen to this.

He moves to leave; she stops him.

SARAH: My father always stood up for my mother, though they had only a country marriage. He honoured her throughout his life. He acknowledged her in his will. He would never have allowed anyone to treat her with disrespect, let alone call her a whore. And then there's you, John Ballenden. Why shouldn't I be shunned and slandered when my own husband has so little faith in me.

BALLENDEN: Sarah—

SARAH: You need to think about that. You need to see what I've been trying to tell you. We're at a point in this place when people like me have to demand respect, or we're going to lose our way. I love you, John, I've always loved you. But you have to stand by me in this. You have to believe in my innocence, no matter what you hear in that courtroom. You have to defend me at every turn. Promise me that. Promise me!

End of Act One.

ACT TWO

Scene 1

The Courtroom. Day Three of the trial. MRS. COCKRAN as witness. THE MAJOR slams the gavel.

FOSS: Please tell the Court who you are.

MRS. COCKRAN: I'm the wife of the Reverend Mr. Cockran.

FOSS: How long have you known Mrs. Ballenden?

MRS. COCKRAN: Oh my, many years. When I first came to Red River I ran a boarding school for girls. It was ever so popular with the Company men. They sent me their country-born daughters to acquire the skills of ladies. Mrs. Ballenden was one of my pupils—an exceptional one, I must say. It was hard to keep ahead of her.

FOSS: You must be proud of her accomplishments.

MRS. COCKRAN: She's risen higher than any of my girls.

FOSS: Has she been kind to you over the years?

MRS. COCKRAN: Kind? Oh my, yes.

FOSS: She nursed you when you were ill, in fact.

MRS. COCKRAN: Oh, when we went through Sault Ste Marie? Yes, I was very ill. She nursed me back to health.

FOSS: Even though she was pregnant.

MRS. COCKRAN: That's true. She was quite far along.

FOSS: Even though your daughters were with you, who might have nursed you themselves.

MRS. COCKRAN: Mrs. Ballenden rather insisted.

FOSS: I'm sure she did. And you sent her a most affectionate letter, thanking her for her kindness. Is that correct?

MRS. COCKRAN: I did write to her, yes.

FOSS: Have you been entertained by Mrs. Ballenden at the Chief Factor's residence since she has presided there?

MRS. COCKRAN: Oh my, often.

FOSS: Yet you recently declined her invitation to lunch. Why?

MRS. COCKRAN: *(Uncomfortable.)* I had my reasons.

FOSS: What were they?

MRS. COCKRAN: I knew the Bishop's sister had declined—

FOSS: So you decided to follow her lead. Even though you've known Mrs. Ballenden all these years, and she's been so kind to you. And often entertained you before.

MRS. COCKRAN: I did feel a little disloyal.

FOSS: A *little* disloyal.

MRS. COCKRAN: I'd been hearing talk, and—

FOSS: From whom?

MRS. COCKRAN: My daily, who'd heard it from one of Mrs. Ballenden's servants.

FOSS: Which one?

MRS. COCKRAN: Mrs. Davidson.

FOSS: What had she heard?

MRS. COCKRAN: That Mrs. Ballenden's behaviour with you was enough to entitle Mr. Ballenden to a divorce.

FOSS: And you believed that.

MRS. COCKRAN: I didn't know whether to believe it or not. I was quite distraught. I consulted my husband, who said that whenever rumours of this kind were in circulation, he has always found them to turn out correct.

FOSS: Thank you. That will be all.

PELLY: Mrs. Cockran. Is it true that you have forbidden your daughters to come anywhere near the Upper Fort?

MRS. COCKRAN: Yes.

PELLY: Why is that?

MRS. COCKRAN: For the sake of their characters.

PELLY: Because of the talk you'd been hearing?

MRS. COCKRAN: *(Reluctantly.)* In part.

THOM: You cannot hint at things, Mrs. Cockran. You must say them straight out.

MRS. COCKRAN: *(Miserable.)* I know. But I hate this trial and everything it stands for. I hate what it says about us. You'd think that no one in Red River had anything to do but gossip. And it isn't true. It's not how we really are. Oh, and I don't like sitting here having to describe something I'd rather not have seen.

PELLY: What was that?

MRS. COCKRAN: I called on Mrs. Ballenden one evening not long ago. She and Captain Foss were in the parlour. They were on the sofa together in a situation I found—indecorous. So much so that I retreated for a moment.

PELLY: What were the Captain and Mrs. Ballenden doing?

MRS. COCKRAN: They were huddled together on the sofa.

SARAH: Huddled.

MRS. COCKRAN: They were smiling and—huddled together.

PELLY: Was there anyone else in the room?

MRS. COCKRAN: No.

BALLENDEN: For God's sake, I'd just stepped out.

THE MAJOR: Mr. Ballenden. Please.

PELLY: *(Delighted.)* Thank you, Mrs. Cockran.

DAVIDSON: Thank you, thank you.

THOM: Mrs. Cockran, a question or two from the Bench. On the occasion you've just described, was Mrs. Ballenden expecting you?

MRS. COCKRAN: No.

THOM: Had you been announced?

MRS. COCKRAN: There was no one about.

THOM: So you simply barged in. Do you consider that appropriate behaviour?

MRS. COCKRAN: Normally, no, but—

THOM: Was the door to the parlour open or closed?

MRS. COCKRAN: I don't remember.

THOM: Please try.

MRS. COCKRAN: *(Considers.)* It must have been open, else I'd have knocked.

THOM: Do you not think that had Mrs. Ballenden and Captain Foss intended to misbehave in her parlour, they would have first shut the door?

MRS. COCKRAN: I wouldn't know. I don't misbehave.

THOM: Except on that occasion, perhaps.

MRS. COCKRAN: That's not fair. I went with the best of intentions. I'd been very hurt by something Mrs. Ballenden had said in front of the Bishop's sister.

THOM: What had she said?

MRS. COCKRAN: She quoted a phrase my husband once used, when he was new to this place. But that was long ago. He would never say it now.

THOM: What was it, exactly?

MRS. COCKRAN: Please don't make me repeat it. It would be very hurtful to many in this room. The point of it is, I felt I deserved an apology.

THOM: Did you get it?

MRS. COCKRAN: Oh, yes. She offered it the moment she saw me.

THOM: As a lady, and a friend, would do. Thank you, Mrs. Cockran.

PELLY: You're neglecting your duties, Mr. Thom.

THOM: I beg your pardon?

PELLY: We've had hearsay and double hearsay and triple hearsay testimony since this trial began. You ought to point out to the jury that what Mrs. Cockran has just disclosed is the first important piece of non-hearsay evidence we've heard. She didn't merely learn from someone else that Mrs. Ballenden and Captain Foss had been engaged in indecorous behaviour; she witnessed it herself. She has sworn to it in Court. You ought to ensure that the jury understands how vital her testimony is to our defence. But you won't, of course you won't, because you're biased in favour of the Plaintiff. I said at the start that this trial was rigged. I say it again. If you think your superiors won't hear of this, you'd better think again.

THOM: Are you threatening me, Mr. Pelly?

PELLY: Simply making a point, Mr. Thom.

THOM: Oh, you're the cock of the walk now, aren't you, Pelly? I suggest that you remember your *place*.

THE MAJOR: That reminds me of a response I once gave to a visitor to Red River. He was from Boston or New York or somewhere and I must say rather irritable. "What is this place?" he muttered. To which I replied, "Place, sir? It's *space*, sir!" I thought that was rather clever. *(Glances around; clears his throat.)* Next witness.

Scene 2

After the trial. Upper Fort. Chief Factor's Residence. Bedroom. SARAH and BALLENDEN.

SARAH: What do you mean, they're moving in?

BALLENDEN: This *is* where the Chief Factor lives.

SARAH: But you withdrew your resignation.

BALLENDEN: I asked Sir George if I could.

SARAH: And?

BALLENDEN: He's thinking about it. In the meantime, someone has to take charge. He's appointed Mr. Black.

SARAH: No, I can't have it. I won't. I can't have Margaret here. And I certainly can't have that husband of hers, with his pompous ways. They'll have to stay in the officer's quarters.

BALLENDEN: I suggested that. I was overruled.

SARAH: But surely even Sir George understands how awkward it would be, the four of us under one roof. The man has no heart at all. Maybe we should move out.

BALLENDEN: I considered that, but I'm afraid if we did I would stand no chance at all of being reinstated.

SARAH: He's punishing us for the trial. He bided his time until it was over, but he'd planned this all along.

BALLENDEN: There you go again. You never give him the benefit of the doubt.

SARAH: Maybe I could if he'd ever once done the same for me.

BALLENDEN: I do not want to argue with you. The Blacks will come up tomorrow from the Lower Fort, and that's all there is to it.

SARAH: Where am I to put them?

BALLENDEN: That's up to you.

SARAH: Is it? Or is it up to Margaret now?

BALLENDEN: *(Exasperated.)* Oh, Sarah, I don't know. *(Takes a breath.)* Given that the situation is temporary, I think we can assume the decision is yours.

SARAH: Well, I'm not giving up my bedroom.

BALLENDEN: I'll give up mine, then, and move in with you.

SARAH: I'm not sure I want you there just now. I'm hurt, and angry with you.

BALLENDEN: Aye, well, I'm not so pleased with you. If you'd told me that Pelly had fallen for you, I would have transferred him out of here. Just think. None of this would have happened.

SARAH: So that's what you've been thinking. That it's all my fault.

BALLENDEN: That is not what I said.

SARAH: I did want to confront the Bishop's sister the moment I knew she'd snubbed me. Maybe if you hadn't advised against it—

BALLENDEN: If, if, if! Are we going to devour each other?

Beat.

SARAH: You say you're not pleased with me. I'm not sure you ever were.

BALLENDEN: What's this, now?

SARAH: There's always been a qualification in your attitude towards me. Not exactly condescension, but—

BALLENDEN: Stop it.

SARAH: Maybe a little embarrassment. When you introduce me to strangers, and read the look in their eyes.

BALLENDEN: *(Takes her by the shoulders.)* Do not do this! Do not let them undermine your confidence. You have to stay strong. If not for yourself, for me.

SARAH: Yes, you need that, don't you. But you're not required to be strong for me.

BALLENDEN: *(Drops his hands.)* Did I not promise to defend you at every turn, and have I not done it? What more do you want of me? You cannot expect me to disobey orders. You do not do that in the Company, or you do not rise. Your children do not get good educations. *You* do not get to wear the finest gowns and throw the most lavish balls.

SARAH: As if I cared about that.

BALLENDEN: You do care about it, do not tell me that. You care about it, Sarah, more than you'd ever admit, else why did you marry me?

SARAH: I married you because I loved you.

BALLENDEN: Aye, and liked what I had to offer.

SARAH: I could say the same about you.

BALLENDEN: But *I* would not deny it.

SARAH: All I ever wanted was to be with you. Sometimes I think if you'd never risen, I'd have my daughters with me now. Gowns and lavish balls. I'd take my girls any day.

BALLENDEN: *(Moves to her, takes her hand.)* Why is it that every quarrel we have eventually comes back to the girls?

SARAH: Because I feel their absence so keenly.

BALLENDEN: *(Beat.)* We were talking about the Blacks, remember?

SARAH: Oh, John. He can't choose Black over you. You're so much the better man. And you don't strut around like you own the place. That doesn't sit well around here. Margaret will be chuffed, of course. There'll be no containing her now. And after what she said in court.

BALLENDEN: I think we should agree not to discuss the trial. It's time to put it behind us.

SARAH: I can't put Margaret behind me.

Scene 3

The Courtroom. Day Three of the trial. MARGARET as witness.

FOSS: Please tell the Court who you are.

MARGARET: I'm Margaret Black, wife of the Chief Trader.

FOSS: Has Mrs. Pelly ever spoken to you about the matter before the Court?

MARGARET: She has. She told me that Mrs. Ballenden had been seen going to your quarters.

FOSS: What else?

MARGARET: She said that Mrs. Davidson had told her that Mrs. Ballenden had given the German girl a gift before she left Red River, a gift so generous that one could conclude that the girl had been bribed. A gold ring, a silk cloak and a dress.

FOSS: What else did Mrs. Pelly tell you?

MARGARET: She said she'd heard that the last child Mrs. Ballenden had was yours.

FOSS: That's a heinous accusation to repeat. But you swear she said that?

MARGARET: I do.

FOSS: Thank you for clarifying for all of us Mrs. Pelly's contribution to this scandal. Were you surprised that such an accusation would be levelled at Mrs. Ballenden?

MARGARET: Not entirely. There's always been talk around Mrs. Ballenden. When she and her husband came back from Sault Ste Marie to take charge of the Upper Fort, one of the English ladies told me that Mrs. Ballenden was the kind of woman who must always have a sweetheart as well as a husband.

FOSS: Why would she say such a thing?

MARGARET: It was by way of a warning, I think. I had recently returned from England after an absence of many years. I suppose she was endeavouring to ensure that I wouldn't be—tainted by association.

SARAH: Traitor.

FOSS: You've known Mrs. Ballenden many years, have you not?

MARGARET: Since we were children.

FOSS: So when you hear this kind of talk about her, what is your response?

MARGARET: I change the topic of conversation as politely as I can, so as not to give offence.

FOSS: In other words, you don't defend her. Thank you, Mrs. Black.

THE MAJOR: Mr. Pelly.

PELLY: Mrs. Black. You attended the dinner hosted by Mr. Harriott several months back. Were the Ballendens present on that occasion?

MARGARET: They were.

PELLY: Was Captain Foss?

MARGARET: No.

PELLY: Did you witness anything that evening that would suggest that the rumours you'd been hearing were true?

MARGARET: I can only describe what I saw.

PELLY: Please do.

MARGARET: Mrs. Ballenden left the room twice—to check on the children, she said. The first time she went with one of the ladies, the second time alone. She was gone about half an hour. I happened to run into the German girl later in the evening. I asked her why Mrs. Ballenden was so anxious about the children. The girl said her mistress had not come near them.

PELLY: The implication being…

MARGARET: Well, if she wasn't with the children, where was she?

THOM: Do you mean to tell us that you pumped Mrs. Ballenden's maid for information about her mistress's whereabouts? And you call yourself a lady.

MARGARET: I don't call myself a lady, Mr. Thom. I *am* a lady.

THOM: Judging by what we've heard from *ladies* in this room, perhaps you are.

Scene 4

After the trial. Lower Fort. A Company office. SIMPSON and BALLENDEN.

BALLENDEN: It's impossible to carry on any longer. It's been nearly a month, Sir George, since the Blacks moved in with us. Mrs. Ballenden and Mrs. Black do not speak to each other. Mr. Black will not acknowledge my wife. Yesterday, the Bishop and his sister came to visit the Blacks. Mrs. Ballenden and I had to hide away like fugitives until they'd gone. It was like a scene from a farce. We have to have a decision, Sir George. Will you or will you not allow me to withdraw my resignation?

SIMPSON: Interesting. Mr. Black was here earlier with the same request. I told him that, considering your experience and your popularity in the settlement, from a business point of view it would be preferable if you were reinstated. I told him that if he would voluntarily give up the position, I would be well pleased.

BALLENDEN: Thank you, Sir George, that's—

SIMPSON: But he refused to do so. He said he did not see why he should be made to suffer for your vacillation. On the whole, I agree with him. I've decided to leave things as they are.

BALLENDEN: *(Beat.)* I see.

SIMPSON: You can move your family here to the Lower Fort. The Ross cottage will be comfortable, I think. How are you feeling these days?

BALLENDEN: Distressed, of course.

SIMPSON: Physically.

BALLENDEN: Stronger.

SIMPSON: Stronger, but certainly not strong. I'm going to give you some advice. I think you should take this opportunity to go back to Scotland and have yourself examined by the finest doctors you can find. You're still a young man, relatively speaking, with a bright career ahead of you…if you show yourself capable of making some tough decisions.

BALLENDEN: What do you mean?

SIMPSON: I think you should go back to Scotland alone—

BALLENDEN: Alone?

SIMPSON: And consider your future. Whether or not it should include your wife. In your shoes, I can tell you, for the honour of the Company if not for my own, I would opt for divorce.

BALLENDEN: Divorce?!

SIMPSON: Divorce, and put all this cleanly behind. By the way, you might as well know: I'm demoting Mr. Thom.

BALLENDEN: Surely that's not necessary.

SIMPSON: I advised him quite strenuously to disengage himself from the trial. He refused to take my advice.

BALLENDEN: You're punishing him for being loyal to me.

SIMPSON: Nonsense. He's worn out his welcome with our friends across the river. Did he not once publicly announce that the only way to save the French was to turn them all into Brits? Besides, there've been complaints up the line.

BALLENDEN: Pelly, you mean. He threatened as much in court. He had it in his head that Mr. Thom was biased against him—

SIMPSON: That will be all, Ballenden.

Scene 5

The Courtroom. Day Three of the trial.

FOSS: I hold in my hand a statement sworn to before witnesses by Mrs. Ballenden's former maid, Catherine Weingart, usually referred to as "the German girl." I'd like it read into the record, please.

THOM: Would you do the honours, Major?

FOSS hands the statement to THE MAJOR.

THE MAJOR: (*Reads, in a thick German accent.*) I, Catherine Weingart, do swear and attest to the following. That I came up with the Ballendens from Sault Ste Marie and have been two years Mrs. Ballenden's personal maid. That I am leaving Red River by my own choice, as it is my dearest wish to return to my mother.

THOM: You can dispense with the accent, Major.

THE MAJOR: Oh, indulge me, Mr. Thom. I'm a thwarted thespian, you know. *(Resumes reading.)* I do also swear and attest that I have been treated always well and kindly by the Ballendens, but I can't say the same for all others. I have been called by Mr. Davidson a Catholic devil.

SARAH: I implore you, Major, to read in your own voice. It's not her fault she had an accent. You're demeaning her.

THE MAJOR: Am I? Very well. *(Without the accent.)* After overhearing Mrs. Davidson and her husband speaking lies about my mistress, I was locked out of the kitchen. Mrs. Pelly gave me gifts for repeating these lies to her. These gifts were a pair of earrings she had tired of and the cheapest of all hairpins. These gifts I leave behind. They put lies on my lips which I did not want and which I am glad to confess.

I finally swear and attest that I have made this statement of my own accord, freely and gladly, so that I leave Red River with a good conscience. *(Stops reading.)* It is signed with an "X" on July tenth, 1850, before three witnesses. It seems to be in order.

PELLY: In order? That's hardly the phrase I'd use.

THOM: Questions, Captain Foss?

FOSS: No. *(To THE MAJOR.)* Thank you, Sir.

THE MAJOR: Mr. Pelly?

PELLY: No.

DAVIDSON: Me neither.

THE MAJOR: Well, that's refreshing. *(Slams the gavel.)* Next witness!

THOM: You're giving me a headache, Major, the way you work that gavel. Please try to restrain yourself.

FOSS: As my next witness, I call Mrs. Ballenden.

Scene 6

After the trial. Red River Settlement. THOM's office. BALLENDEN and THOM.

THOM: Thank you for stopping in. I felt sure you'd want to know. The community is rallying behind you. The Council has drawn up a petition and got five hundred signatures. They're calling on Sir George to reinstate you as Chief Factor.

BALLENDEN: That's wonderful news. Five hundred!

THOM: They could have got more, but time is pressing. They want a decision before he leaves, and that can't be long. It's nearly September. *(Beat.)* I do not like to see you so low.

BALLENDEN: I blame myself, you see.

THOM: My friend—

BALLENDEN: She's always been independent, outspoken. I've mostly not minded that. But I wonder if, through my faith in her, or what might be called my negligence, I've put her in harm's way.

THOM: Nonsense. You must not think that.

BALLENDEN: It gets a bit muddy, though, does it not? Where is the high moral ground? I do not feel I can rightfully ascend to that.

THOM: Why would you say such a thing?

BALLENDEN: *(Hesitates.)* My father was also a Company man. He came out as an indentured servant and rose to be Chief Factor at York. I was very proud of him, but then—*(Breaks off.)* Well, you know, Mr. Thom—I'm sure you've deduced—I have some half-brothers about.

THOM: It's the way of things here. Did your mother know?

BALLENDEN: It would have killed her. She was forever writing letters to the Company, begging them to give my father furlough. How humiliated she'd have been if she'd known—as the Company very well did—that he was happily settled on the Bay with a woman named Jane. I knew none of this until I joined the Company and came out myself. It was an awful shock.

THOM: Aye.

BALLENDEN: So I cannot hold the high moral ground. After all, there's my father. And I would not have Sarah, would I?—had her father, and her grandfather, for that matter—not loved native women. On the other hand…well, you know Sir George.

THOM: In these matters, my friend, and between these walls, Sir George is a hypocrite.

BALLENDEN: What I wouldn't give to quit the Company. Take her away from all this. I dream of taking her home, you know, her and the little ones. Gathering my family together. It's hard to be parted from your children. It wears greatly on Sarah, so I try to pretend that it does not also wear greatly on me. But it does. It does.

THOM: Why not do it, then? Quit, and be out of this.

BALLENDEN: I'm not a rich man, Mr. Thom. I may be one day, with the Company shares. Until then I must carry the burden. *(Beat.)* Mrs. Ballenden will be delighted to hear about the petition. Thank you for telling me.

Scene 7

After the trial. Upper Fort. Chief Factor's Residence. Bedroom. SARAH alone. FLORA enters.

FLORA: Mrs. Ballenden?

SARAH: Yes, Flora.

FLORA: When you leave the Upper Fort, take me with you, please.

SARAH: What makes you think I'm leaving?

FLORA: Mrs. Black's been telling everyone.

SARAH: Telling them what?

FLORA: That her husband's to remain as Chief Factor. That you and Mr. Ballenden and the children are being sent to the Lower Fort. She's all puffed up about it.

SARAH: But—the petition.

FLORA: I want to go with you, Mrs. Ballenden. I can't work for her. She's no more English than I am but you'd never know it, the airs she puts on. And it's only going to get worse. I despise her for what she said in Court. She betrayed us all when she betrayed you. I don't care what you make me do, make me the scullery maid. I won't complain, and I'll never gossip. I'll be loyal to you for as long as you need me.

SARAH: Flora…I don't know what to say. I'm touched. But you're still so young. It's quiet at the Lower Fort. Boring, even.

FLORA: I don't mind about that. You were good to my grandmother. I know she'd want me to stand by you.

SARAH: You must miss her, Flora.

FLORA: I miss what she used to be. Funny, and warm, and full of stories. But I'm glad she's gone home, for her sake.

SARAH: Let me check with Mr. Ballenden.

FLORA: Thank you.

FLORA exits. BALLENDEN enters.

BALLENDEN: Sarah, I have bad news.

SARAH: He ignored the petition.

BALLENDEN: You heard.

SARAH: He thinks he's a god, that's why. He has no respect for any of us. Every man who signed it should be up in arms. Now we have no choice. We have to move.

BALLENDEN: To the Lower Fort.

SARAH: With him in residence there.

BALLENDEN: He's leaving in a day or so.

SARAH: Thank God for that. *Where* in the Lower Fort?

BALLENDEN: The Ross cottage.

SARAH: The Ross cottage. We'll be tripping over each other.

BALLENDEN: It's rather pretty, I think.

SARAH: The children will miss their friends. *(Paces.)* I'd like to be allowed to choose my staff.

BALLENDEN: There'd be no objection to that.

SARAH: Though heaven knows where I'll put them.

BALLENDEN: I presume in the Big House, in the servants' quarters.

SARAH: You presume.

BALLENDEN: Please. Do not make this any harder for me than it already is.

SARAH: It's like being banished. It *is* being banished. That man has passed judgment on me. He's tried me in the court of his mind and found me guilty.

BALLENDEN: Sarah—

SARAH: He has. He found me guilty the moment he heard what Pelly and the others had said. Then he bullied you into resigning. After all the good work you've done. In spite of the fact that you've risked your health for the sake of the Company.

BALLENDEN: It may turn out for the best. We've had no privacy here. Our names on every tongue. It might be good for both of us to be left alone for a while. Out of sight, out of mind. *(Takes her hand.)* Give me a smile, sweetheart. It could always be worse.

SARAH: If we have to move, let's get on with it.

Scene 8

After the trial. Upper Fort. THE MAJOR's office. THE MAJOR and FOSS.

THE MAJOR: I'm not going to beat about the bush. You've been recalled. You're to return to England as soon as possible.

FOSS: You can't be serious.

THE MAJOR hands FOSS a letter, which he scans.

What about my land? Am I to walk away from that?

THE MAJOR: I couldn't say.

FOSS: You couldn't say. You know very well 'twas the land I came for. I fully intended to stay.

THE MAJOR: No one's saying you can't stay. If you resign your commission.

FOSS: I can't resign my commission! I need the income.

THE MAJOR: Well then, you have a problem.

FOSS: *(Throws the letter down.)* This is because of the trial. Someone's had a word with the War Office.

THE MAJOR: In case you're wondering, it wasn't me.

FOSS: Of course it wasn't you. Why would they listen to *you*? It was someone high up in the Company. And look what it's cost me, look what it's cost me! My land, my future, my children's future. And you stand there looking smug.

THE MAJOR: Why shouldn't I? You wouldn't know a principle if you tripped over it. You're a gambler, a poser, a spendthrift, and probably an adulterer. If you weren't entertaining Mrs. Ballenden in your quarters, who were you entertaining? I don't even want to know.

FOSS: I don't suppose you ever heard the griping in the settlement after you arrived. They'd been told to expect a fine, clever man with a commanding presence. And what did they get? A dim-witted buffoon.

THE MAJOR: Listen to me. I don't give a fiddler's fart whether you stay or go. Just get the hell out of your quarters. I'll need them for your replacement.

FOSS: And who is that?

THE MAJOR: I wouldn't know yet, would I?

FOSS: I hope he can work with you, whoever the poor bugger is. God knows, no one else can. Incompetent ass.

THE MAJOR: I'm still your commanding officer. I'll have you up for insubordination.

FOSS: Sure, sure.

THE MAJOR: I shall have you up!

FOSS exits, laughing.

Scene 9

The Courtroom. Day Three of the trial. SARAH as witness.

FOSS: Mrs. Ballenden. Can you think of any reason why Mr. Pelly would want to damage your reputation or endanger your happiness?

SARAH: When Mr. Pelly first came to Red River, the autumn before he was married, he often came to me for Company medicine. On one occasion he told me that, had he known the society he'd be in at Red River, he would not have become engaged. That if the intended Mrs. Pelly did not soon come out, it was a marriage that wouldn't happen.

PELLY: *(To SARAH.)* Thanks very much. My wife must love hearing that.

SARAH: *(To PELLY.)* It's what you said.

FOSS: Go on, Mrs. Ballenden.

SARAH: On another occasion, he told me that, having met me, he understood why there was some—disparaging talk about me within the Company. He said—*(Breaks off.)* This is embarrassing.

FOSS: Please tell us, Mrs. Ballenden.

SARAH: He said it was envy. He said something like—women envy you your beauty, and men envy the other men your eyes fall on.

FOSS: Were you surprised to learn there was ill talk about you?

SARAH: No. I feel I've been scrutinized—over-scrutinized—ever since my marriage.

FOSS: Go on.

SARAH: The next day Mr. Harriott came to see me. He asked to speak to me as a friend. He said that Mr. Pelly was a very vain young man and that I should be on my guard as to how I conducted myself towards him. He said Mr. Pelly had confessed to him that, given the chance, he would gladly run away with me.

FOSS: What did you do then?

SARAH: I took the first opportunity to put Mr. Pelly in his place. I told him I'd heard what he'd said and that I would never regard him as anything other than my husband's accountant. I've maintained that line of conduct with him ever since.

FOSS: Did you tell Mr. Ballenden what had happened?

SARAH: Not at the time. He was still recovering from his stroke. The doctors had said he was not on any account to be upset, and it would have greatly upset him. I finally told him a few nights ago to prepare him for my testimony.

FOSS: The Major has testified that Mr. Pelly told him that you once placed your hand on his thigh. Did you?

SARAH: Certainly not.

FOSS: You're sure?

SARAH: I have never placed my hand on Mr. Pelly's thigh.

FOSS: Not even by accident?

SARAH: Not by accident, not deliberately, not ever.

FOSS: What is your relationship with Mrs. Pelly?

SARAH: We have no relationship now.

FOSS: And before?

SARAH: I did my best to make her feel welcome when she first arrived. It's often a difficult adjustment. She made it clear from the outset that she didn't intend to call on my advice or assistance.

FOSS: She didn't intend to *kowtow* to you.

SARAH: That's how she put it, yes.

FOSS: Can you think of any reason your mess cook or your scullery maid would speak against you?

THOM: Mr. Davidson, you may wish to wake up. This testimony bears on your character and on that of your wife.

DAVIDSON: *(Rouses himself.)* Yes, sir. I shall give it my full attention, sir. Much obliged. Sir.

SARAH: I don't believe I've ever given Mr. Davidson reason to speak against me.

FOSS: And his wife?

SARAH: I agreed to employ Mrs. Davidson at the Upper Fort because Mr. Davidson prevailed upon me. He wanted her there with him. I knew of her reputation, so I—

FOSS: What reputation is that?

SARAH hesitates.

Allow me say it for you. She's known to be a gossip.

THOM: Is that a fair comment, Mr. Davidson?

DAVIDSON: I can't deny it, sir. I've warned her often enough. I told her she'd have us out of a job if she didn't mind her mouth.

SARAH: So I placed her where she might do the least harm. She's made it clear by her behaviour in my presence that she was disappointed in my decision.

FOSS: In other words, she bore a grudge.

DAVIDSON: Why wouldn't she? She gave up a very good position to be made a scullery maid. Upstairs maid she was, lace collar and all. I was ever so disappointed to see her brought so low.

THOM: Where's that bloody gavel when we need it?

THE MAJOR: *(Slams the gavel.)* Silence!

FOSS: *(To SARAH.)* Mrs. Black has testified that on the night of the dinner hosted by Mr. Harriott, you left the room alone to check on your children. She questioned the German girl, who said you hadn't come near them.

SARAH: I can't explain why Catherine would say that. I did look in on them twice that evening. My youngest had a fever. I was concerned about her.

FOSS: I have one more question, Mrs. Ballenden. 'Tis a difficult one, but I'm afraid I must put it to you. Dr. Bunn has testified that your husband told him that during your last pregnancy you suggested that the two of you separate. Why would you make a suggestion like that?

SARAH: I've borne six children. It would be one thing if I could have them with me. But my eldest are away at school, and the younger ones will follow. I've bowed to my husband's wishes in this, but not always graciously. Sometimes I lash out. He understands why I do.

FOSS: Thank you, Mrs. Ballenden. That will be all.

THOM: Your witness, Mr. Pelly.

PELLY: *(To SARAH.)* I'd like to start by questioning you about the German girl.

DAVIDSON: Good on you.

SARAH: Her name is Catherine.

PELLY: On her *timely* departure from the settlement, you gave her a gift. What was it for?

SARAH: For her kindness to my children.

PELLY: A gold ring, a silk cloak and a dress. Some would consider that a most extravagant gift from a mistress to a maid, no matter how kind she was. Some would consider it unseemly.

SARAH: Unseemly?

PELLY: In poor taste.

SARAH: I know what the word means.

PELLY: If so, then perhaps you can understand why others might construe such a gift as payment for something other than mere kindness.

SARAH: If I could control how others choose to construe my actions, I wouldn't be sitting here now.

PELLY: She was your personal maid and would have been privy to your comings and goings. She told others that you went to the Captain's quarters. She said she was sometimes set to watch, to make excuses to your husband should he miss you. We've heard these statements as testimony in Court. How do you respond?

SARAH: They are lies.

PELLY: You'd employ someone in an intimate position who would spread such lies about you?

SARAH: You heard her statement. She was bullied, and bribed into saying things she knew weren't true. She was relieved to be able to confess it.

PELLY: She confessed to lying, Mrs. Ballenden. Yet you'd have us believe that she was bullied by the Davidsons and bribed by my wife, a lady of impeccable reputation. You'd actually have us believe that.

THOM: Watch your tone, Mr. Pelly.

PELLY: (*To THOM.*) Yes, you would defend her. But my wife has been accused of bribery. I do not intend to leave this room until it is written into the record that this monstrous accusation was made by a self-confessed liar.

THOM: *(Grim.)* Fine.

PELLY: After all, my wife is not allowed to testify. She can't defend herself, any more than I can. I have to sit here and listen to my relationship with Mrs. Ballenden portrayed to her best advantage.

THOM: Mr. Pelly—

PELLY: No mention of her flirtatiousness. No mention of the gestures, the smiles, the glances she cast my way that were clearly meant to entice.

SARAH: Entice?!

PELLY: No mention of her hand brushing mine on a certain evening at mess or the toe of her shoe on mine under the table at cards. I'm not allowed to establish—

BALLENDEN: *(Stands.)* Pelly, for the love of God—

PELLY: —that she in fact led me on in the most blatant manner!

SARAH: *(Leaps to her feet.)* That's a lie!

PELLY: Oh, she can deny it, but a man knows by the look in a woman's eye—

SARAH: I can't listen to this!

FOSS: *(To PELLY.)* You son of a bitch!

FOSS hurls himself at PELLY. A fistfight ensues. There are shouts from the other characters.

THE MAJOR: *(Slams the gavel.)* Order! Order!

BALLENDEN takes hold of FOSS, DAVIDSON grabs PELLY. The fighters are pulled apart.

PELLY: You'll pay for this, Foss.

FOSS: The hell I will.

PELLY: I'll make you bloody pay.

FOSS: I'll see you in the grave first, you pathetic piece of—

PELLY: Bastard!

THE MAJOR: Mr. Pelly! That's enough out of you. As for you, Captain, I would ask you to remember, if you ever knew, that you're an officer of the British army. Conduct yourself accordingly.

THOM: This has been a great strain on all of us. I suggest we call a recess.

FOSS: First! First. I propose a settlement. It should be clear to the Court by now that Mrs. Ballenden has been the victim of vicious lies. If the Defendants agree to the Court declaring her innocent of the accusations against her, I'll forego my claim to damages and we'll call it a day.

DAVIDSON: Done!

PELLY: I'll accept that settlement only if Captain Foss agrees to acknowledge my innocence, and the innocence of my wife, with regard to the rumours that have circulated about him and Mrs. Ballenden.

FOSS: Acknowledge your innocence? Out of the question.

PELLY: Then we proceed.

DAVIDSON: *(In utter frustration.)* Aw, Mr. Pelly—!

Scene 10

After the trial. Red River Settlement. Anglican Church. The BISHOP is in the pulpit, wearing lavender-coloured leather gloves.

BISHOP: My friends. I left the settlement some weeks ago to serve the larger parish. I went away confident in the good will and charity of the people to whom I'd return. Imagine my dismay to find instead, what? Chaos and upheaval. A community divided unto itself, neighbour against neighbour. Instead of kindly greetings, one man to another, what? Quarrels in the streets. Instead of gentle smiles between the women, silence and bitter looks. Ill will at every turn. Now, as your Bishop, I urge you to put aside these base emotions and embrace one another once again in friendship and tolerance. Remind yourselves that all of us are, what? Human, and therefore prone to sin. Find it in your hearts to forgive those amongst you who succumb to moral depravity. No jury, no jury's verdict, can cancel out such sins. These are for God to judge. Find it in your hearts to forgive those who, in blatant disregard of the divisions they would sow in the community, chose to flaunt their depravity through the medium of a public trial. Make up your minds forevermore to close your ears to gossip and open them to the Lord. For as ye judge, so shall ye be judged. In the name of the Father, and the Son, and the Holy Ghost…

Scene 11

After the trial. Lower Fort. Ross Cottage. Parlour. SARAH, BALLENDEN, THOM.

THOM: It's that wasp of a sister. She put him up to it, and he was fool enough to comply. I tell you, it's intolerable. It's the interference of gospel with law. If he thinks the place was divided before, he should take a look now. He's driven a wedge between the clergy and the community that's as wide as that river out there. It's most vexing. Enough to turn you Methodist. Forgive me for ranting.

BALLENDEN: Not at all. The man should be defrocked, and sent home in disgrace. *(Beat.)* Are you going to be all right, Mr. Thom?

THOM: Now that I've been demoted? Oh, I expect so. I managed to hang onto the whole of my salary.

BALLENDEN: Thank God for that.

SARAH: I'm so sorry, Mr. Thom.

THOM: Nothing for you to be sorry for. I make my own choices, always. And on that note, I'll say goodbye and wend my way back to the settlement.

SARAH: I wish we could offer to put you up overnight.

THOM: No need, no need. I enjoy a ride on a crisp autumn day. It was lovely to see you, Mrs. Ballenden. Don't let that sermon get you down. Well, good day to you both.

BALLENDEN: Good day, Mr. Thom. Thank you.

SARAH: Good day.

THOM exits. Children's voices are heard, off, calling their goodbyes to him.

THOM: *(Off.)* Goodbye, children. Goodbye.

Beat.

BALLENDEN: We've come to a pretty pass, have we not?

SARAH: Better days will come.

BALLENDEN: You're right about this place. There isn't room for the children, let alone the servants. Let alone us.

SARAH: It has its advantages. I know where the little ones are all the time. I don't worry half as much.

BALLENDEN: Hmm.

SARAH: Something's bothering you.

BALLENDEN: *(Hesitates.)* The thing is, you see…

SARAH: Just say it.

BALLENDEN: There's something we need to discuss. You must promise not to get angry.

SARAH: I don't like the sound of that.

BALLENDEN: Sir George has suggested that I use this furlough to see to my health in Scotland. It's an opportunity that may not come again soon. I've been thinking I should take it.

SARAH: If you're well enough for the journey.

BALLENDEN: I'd have to be.

SARAH: Oh! To think of seeing my girls! After all this time! And they could come back with us, if you—if—

He moves away.

What's wrong?

BALLENDEN: If you came with me, we'd have to take the little ones. I do not have the strength for that.

SARAH: But—

BALLENDEN: I could manage Johnny. I could take him and get him settled at school. More I could not handle. It's time he was going anyway.

SARAH: I wonder why I keep having them if they must all be sent away.

BALLENDEN: I asked you not to get angry. I'll go nowhere if you'd rather I stayed.

SARAH: Don't put the decision on *me*.

BALLENDEN: Well then, we must make it together. On the one hand, there's my health. In the long run, looking after it is best for all of us. On the other hand, you'd be on your own until spring.

SARAH: They'll say you've abandoned me.

BALLENDEN: They'll say what they like, we know that.

SARAH: They'll say that a man like John Ballenden would never walk out on his wife. Not unless she deserved it. They'll point to your absence as proof. It won't be like it was when that cad McTavish—

BALLENDEN: This again!

SARAH: Walked out on Nancy. Everyone was incensed on her behalf. They won't be incensed for *me*.

BALLENDEN: You always come back to that. It's as though you wish it on yourself.

SARAH: Wish it? I've feared it, I've feared it.

BALLENDEN: That settles it. I'm staying. To hell with my health. To hell with Sir George. You wear me out, Sarah, I swear to God. You wear me out.

SARAH: *(Beat.)* Sir George. I might have known. He told you to leave me behind. Why?

BALLENDEN: You will not forgive him if I tell you.

SARAH: Who cares about *him*?!

BALLENDEN: You will not forgive *me*. *(Beat.)* He thinks I should divorce you. I will not, of course, I would never! But I have to go through the motions of—pretending I might. Appearing to consider it. I want what's best for us, you know that. But sometimes you have to—you can't always… I cannot bear to have you look at me like that. I cannot bear it, Sarah!

SARAH: Everyone in the Company will know why you've gone. Sir George will see to that. He's never approved of me. He'd be delighted to break us apart. And you're going to give him the satisfaction of *appearing to consider it*. A man who's fathered children from one sea to the other. Who's never once in all his life allowed himself to be wrong. You're prepared to bend to such a man.

He thrusts his way out of the room. She shouts after him.

He wouldn't do this if I was white! *(Grabs something to hurl at him.)* You know it. You know it!

Scene 12

After Day Three of the trial. THOM's office. SARAH sits. BALLENDEN paces.

SARAH: Four hours! Is that good or bad, I wonder?

BALLENDEN: At least it's over. We can start to get our lives back.

THOM and FOSS burst in.

THOM: Mr. and Mrs. Ballenden—

FOSS: We won!

THOM: Resoundingly. You asked for a definitive statement, Mrs. Ballenden. You got it. The jury found the defendants guilty and awarded the Captain damages. And the damages—

FOSS: Three hundred pounds from Pelly and a hundred from Davidson.

THOM: Though the Captain graciously told the Court he would not collect from Davidson.

FOSS: It would break him. But I'll gladly take Pelly's money. You've been vindicated, Mrs. Ballenden. Your good name has been restored.

BALLENDEN: Thank God.

SARAH: Oh John, just think. What a story we'll have for our grandchildren!

THOM: *(To SARAH.)* I never doubted your innocence. Now no one can. Oh, I tell you, I'm pleased as punch. We shall have a drink! *(Pours drinks.)* And to think that every question put by the defendants was dealt with. That every piece of hearsay was received. That no slandering man or woman in the settlement was refused the chance to come and throw dirt on you. *(Hands out glasses.)* Well, they came and threw their dirt, but by God none of it stuck, unless it was to them. Well! I'd have bet a pack of martins against a barrel of blubber that we'd get this outcome, but—I tell you, I'm pleased as punch. To justice!

OTHERS: To justice!

They all drink.

BALLENDEN: To Captain Foss!

THOM: Aye, who may well have missed his calling.

FOSS: That's high praise indeed. To Mr. Thom for his guidance!

SARAH: To John Ballenden, for standing by me!

THOM: To the fairest flower of Rupert's land—Sarah Ballenden!

THE MEN: Sarah Ballenden!

They drink.

Scene 13

After the trial. Lower Fort. Ross cottage. Afternoon. SARAH alone. FLORA enters, with tea and a birthday cake.

FLORA: I've brought you tea—and a birthday cake. *(Sets it down.)* It *is* the 10th of December.

SARAH: Thank you, Flora. You're so good to me. Where are the children?

FLORA: Out playing some game they've invented. It seems to involve sticks and chunks of ice and lots of rolling in the snow. I'll call them in a minute.

SARAH: Do you know what I'd like for my birthday? For you to take a few days off. Go back to Red River. Have some fun.

FLORA: I hate Red River.

SARAH: You don't.

FLORA: I do. They should have come and apologized. All the whites. You deserve an apology, you deserve to have your innocence acknowledged, you deserve to be welcomed back. But they won't do it. They won't let any half-breed jury tell them they were wrong. It's the same old buffalo shit.

SARAH: You said it.

FLORA: I'd like to make pemmican out of all of them.

SARAH: Thank God I have you, and the little ones. You've kept me sane. Thank God for your grandmother's courage. I have needed that.

A knock is heard, off.

What's that?

FLORA: There's someone at the door.

FLORA exits.

SARAH: I'd nearly forgotten that sound.

FLORA returns, followed by FOSS.

FLORA: Captain Foss to see you.

SARAH: Captain Foss!

FOSS: I came by a roundabout route. *(Moves to her.)* I don't believe anyone saw me.

FLORA exits.

SARAH: How good to see you, Captain.

FOSS: *(Bows over her hand.)* Mrs. Ballenden.

SARAH: It's a cold day to come so far, but I'm delighted you did. It's been so long since I've seen you. Since the last day of the trial.

FOSS: I wanted to come as soon as I—*(Breaks off.)* Months ago. I was afraid to set the tongues wagging.

SARAH: One thing about the Lower Fort, there aren't many tongues to wag. Can I offer you cake? It's my birthday.

FOSS: Many happy returns.

SARAH: I was born and married in the same month, December. I expect I'll die in December, just to round things out. Seriously, birthday cake?

FOSS: 'Tis enough just to look at you.

SARAH: Sit down, Captain, please.

FOSS: I can't stay long, I'm afraid.

SARAH: Tell me what's happening with you. *(She sits.)*

FOSS: *(Sits.)* I gave up my commission, I suppose you heard.

SARAH: I'm sorry.

FOSS: I had to choose between that and returning to England immediately. I chose to stay, because of the land. Since then we've been fighting about what it's worth. Mr. Black offered to pay me for equipment and produce but not for improvements I've made, and that's the lion's share. We went to arbitration, but that went badly. So I've made a decision. I wanted you to hear it from my lips. I'll be leaving the first chance I get.

SARAH: Leaving.

FOSS: To take it up in London. I'll get nowhere with Black, that's obvious to me now.

SARAH: You're going back.

FOSS: That's right.

SARAH: Permanently.

FOSS: I won't see Red River again, if that's what you mean.

SARAH: But your land, you said—

FOSS: All I can do now is try to convince the Company to pay me what it's worth. I've shocked you, I think. I'm sorry. The only way I could think to tell you was—to tell you.

SARAH: It's all gone, isn't it? Your dream of bringing your family out—

FOSS: Ah, but I'm a gambler at heart. You've always known that. The cards fall this way, the cards fall that way. If the Company deals honourably with me, I won't come out too badly. *(Takes her hands.)* The one thing you can't do, must never do, is blame yourself. I want you to promise me that. I'd do it all again, you know.

SARAH: You can't possibly mean that.

FOSS: I would. You mustn't think otherwise.

SARAH: Thank you for saying that, Captain.

FOSS: Captain. Sure, after all we've been through, you might call me Christopher.

SARAH: Then you must call me Sarah. *(Draws her hands away.)* Though it hardly matters now. Are we really not to see each other, ever again?

FOSS: *(Beat.)* I must say, you look very well. I expected to find you pale and wan. You're positively blooming.

SARAH: I usually am in the first few months.

FOSS: You're in the family way.

SARAH: Flora's grandmother once told me that in the old days, women never had more babies than they could grab and run with if they had to. And look at me.

FOSS: Does he know?

SARAH: He will when he gets my letter.

FOSS: Astonishing, him abandoning you.

SARAH: I knew that's what they'd say. He went home to see to his health. With my complete concurrence.

FOSS: Of course.

SARAH: He is our mainstay, after all.

She stands. FOSS stands.

Oh, why should I lie to you? He's gone home to see to his health, it's true, but also to make a choice. Between his career, and me.

FOSS: Impossible. He said that?

SARAH: We parted on the worst of terms. He took my Johnny with him, to get him in school over there. My dear, brave little man. And I'm stuck out here, all on my own. And I'm pregnant. Again. It should be comic. I should be rolling on the floor, weeping with laughter. And meanwhile—it can't have escaped your notice—all the ones who conspired against us have done very well for themselves. And you, look at all you've lost. And us. And us.

FOSS: Is he coming back?

SARAH: In June, if all goes well.

FOSS: Will you take him back, when he does?

SARAH: *(Moves away.)* Now, that's an interesting question. I've hardly dared raise it myself. All I've wanted since the day we met was simply to be at his side. But now it feels as though something has shifted. And I don't know where it leaves me. *(Faces him.)* What will you do after London, Captain? Christopher.

FOSS: I'll pick up another commission. I hear they're looking for officers on the convict ships to Australia. I may sign on for that. I fancy a warmer place. Do you, Sarah?

SARAH: I like the way you say my name.

FOSS: Do you?

SARAH: Do I what?

FOSS: Fancy a warmer place. I'd take you with me, you know.

SARAH: *(Confused.)* Where?

FOSS: To Australia. I'd take you along in a minute, or send for you.

SARAH: But your wife, your children.

He stares at her, but doesn't answer.

And *my* children, what about them? Oh, but should we? Should we just run off to Australia and be done with all this for all time? Why not, Christopher. Imagine—just imagine the scandal!

They laugh.

FOSS: Would you allow me to kiss you, Sarah? Just the once?

An extended silence sits between them.

SARAH: On the cheek.

He does as instructed, then takes her hands again.

FOSS: I don't want you to despair. There's always a way out if you look hard enough. You must never feel trapped. I would hate to think of you that way. 'Twouldn't become you at all. You must always be that grand, bold creature you were the day we met.

SARAH: God, how I'm going to miss you.

FOSS: And I you. 'Tis the curse of the Irish, you know. We're far too sentimental. I must go.

SARAH: Don't go.

FOSS: *(Pulls away.)* And you must help me to. Send me away without any tears. And remember my offer. Australia! It stands, Sarah, it stands.

Scene 14

The following June. Lower Fort. Ross Cottage. The garden. DR. BUNN enters with a blanket and a cradle. He spreads the blanket on the ground and sets the cradle on it. FLORA enters, carrying a baby and singing a lullaby. DR. BUNN exits. FLORA sits on the blanket. SARAH enters slowly and takes the baby from FLORA, who exits, still singing. SARAH sits with the baby. BALLENDEN enters and kneels next to her.

BALLENDEN: What did you name him?

SARAH: William.

BALLENDEN: He looks like a William, all right. Was it difficult?

SARAH: Yes.

BALLENDEN: I'm sorry. I would not have gone if I'd even suspected—*(Breaks off.)* Where are the others?

SARAH: Flora took them off somewhere. They won't be long.

BALLENDEN: How are you feeling?

SARAH: *(Puts the baby in the cradle.)* Weak.

BALLENDEN: I ran into Dr. Bunn. He's very concerned about you. He says that on top of everything else you have a worrisome cough.

SARAH: I do.

BALLENDEN: What does he prescribe?

SARAH: Rest. But how can I, with a newborn and three little ones?

BALLENDEN: I'll find more help right away. Sarah?

SARAH: Good. *(Beat.)* How are the—?

BALLENDEN: *(Overlapping.)* How are the—?

SARAH: Children?

BALLENDEN: Johnny is settling in well. The girls are lovely, both of them. Annie looks so much like you, it took me aback when I saw her. Eliza has grown very tall. They waltz like true English ladies. But they cannot do the Red River jig like their mother, and that's a great shame. They send their love. *(Takes a bundle from his pocket.)* And letters, of course. *(Hands them to her.)* They miss you very much.

SARAH clasps the letters to her breast.

Are you not going to ask what the doctors had to say?

SARAH: I'm afraid to.

BALLENDEN: They pronounced me cured. They took no credit for it, though. The credit, they said, goes to you, for the care you gave me after my stroke.

SARAH: They really pronounced you cured.

BALLENDEN: They did. They ran a whole battery of tests through the fall. I got the results at Christmas.

SARAH: Christmas. Now it's June.

BALLENDEN: I could not have come back any sooner, you know that very well. Though I longed to. I did long to, Sarah. I missed you, more every day.

He sits next to her on the blanket.

I'm sure you've been lonely.

SARAH: I have.

BALLENDEN: Does no one—has no one called?

SARAH: Captain Foss came to say goodbye. One day, for just a few minutes. But someone saw him leave the Lower Fort, and the gossip started all over again. Ask Mr. Thom, he heard it. No, we're not awash in callers.

Beat.

BALLENDEN: I have a gift for you, Sarah, one that I hope will be worthy of such a wife as you've been to me.

BALLENDEN takes a rectangular jewellery box from his pocket, gives it to SARAH. She opens it.

I had to have it the moment I saw it.

SARAH: I have nothing to wear it with.

BALLENDEN: Then we must get you something. A dress like the one you wore at the ball, when I first laid eyes on you. It was the colour of emeralds, remember? I was only a lowly clerk, but you—

SARAH: *(Hands back the box.)* This won't do at all.

BALLENDEN: But it's an emerald.

SARAH: No, this won't do at all.

She stands with difficulty. He also stands.

You can't come back after nine long months and act as though nothing has changed. It's all changed, John, all of it. *(Moves away.)* Tell me your plans.

BALLENDEN: My orders—

SARAH: Not your orders, your plans. I want to know what you're planning to do about us.

BALLENDEN: I'm going to look after you.

SARAH: In what way?

BALLENDEN: In what way? As my wife.

SARAH: As your legitimate wife, who has never deceived you.

BALLENDEN: If you need me to say it.

SARAH: I do.

BALLENDEN: As my legitimate wife, who has never deceived me. I want you at my side for the rest of my life. I want never to be parted again.

SARAH: *(Beat.)* Did you tell Sir George?

BALLENDEN: I did.

SARAH: And he didn't demote you. Imagine that.

BALLENDEN: Quite the opposite. I should tell you—

SARAH: Just a minute. I've agreed to nothing yet.

BALLENDEN: I beg your pardon?

SARAH: I must have my girls with me. I must have them all. I want to prepare them for the world they'll be living in. The real world, where women with a little more chalk in their skin think somehow that makes them better. I want to teach them to hold their heads high. No one can do it but me. If you have to send my sons away—if you *have to*—I shall learn to bear it. But I must have my girls.

BALLENDEN: I understand.

SARAH: You have to agree.

BALLENDEN: As a matter of principle.

SARAH: Principle. I want your promise, I want your word, I want your commitment to this.

BALLENDEN: As soon as we're settled. I promise you, as soon as we're settled, you shall have your girls.

SARAH: *(Beat.)* Thank you.

BALLENDEN: Unfortunately—

SARAH: I know. I know your orders. Mr. Thom got wind of them. Chief Factor at Fort Vancouver. He never gives up, Sir George. He couldn't separate us legally, so he's doing it physically.

BALLENDEN: I want you there with me, you and the little ones. But you'll have to be strong, much stronger than now. It's hard, going over the mountains, especially for women and children, and we can't leave later than August. Can you be better by then?

SARAH: What I wouldn't give to be able to say yes. The truth is, I don't see how. I can't imagine taking the children all that distance. Not the way I feel now.

BALLENDEN: We'll have to cure you, that's all. We'll get right down to that. *(Picks up the jewellery box.)* May I finish it now? The lovely line I was about to say, before I was interrupted. That I honed all the way from Stromness. *(Fastens the necklace on her neck.)* It reminds me, this necklace does, of the dress you wore at the Chief Factor's ball when I first laid eyes on you. It was the colour of emeralds. I was just a lowly clerk, but you swept into the room in your emerald gown and laid waste to my coward's heart.

SARAH: John. *(Takes his face in her hands.)* You were never a coward. Be with me.

They cling to one another. End of play.

Appendix I

Projections Used in the Premiere Production

Act One	
Scene 1:	July 1850. Red River Settlement. Day One of the Trial.
Scene 2:	Chief Factor's Residence. Before the Trial.
Scene 3:	The Courtroom. Day One of the Trial.
Scene 4:	Chief Factor's Residence. Before the Trial.
Scene 5:	No projection.
Scene 6:	Chief Factor's Residence. Before the Trial.
Scene 7:	No projection.
Scene 8:	Thom's Office. Before the Trial.
Scene 9:	Chief Factor's Residence. Before the Trial.
Scene 10:	Lower Fort. A Company Office. Day One of the Trial.
Scene 11:	Later, Day One of the Trial. Chief Factor's Residence.
Scene 12:	Day Two of the Trial.
Scene 13:	After Day Two of the Trial.
Act Two	
Scene 1:	Day Three of the Trial.
Scene 2:	Chief Factor's Residence. After the Trial.
Scene 3:	No projection.
Scene 4:	After the Trial. Lower Fort. A Company Office.
Scene 5:	No projection.
Scene 6:	Thom's office. After the Trial.
Scene 7:	Chief Factor's Residence. After the Trial.
Scene 8:	Upper Fort. The Major's office. After the Trial.
Scene 9:	No projection.
Scene 10:	Anglican Church. After the Trial.
Scene 11:	Lower Fort. Ross Cottage.
Scene 12:	Thom's office. After Day Three of the Trial.
Scene 13:	Lower Fort. Ross Cottage.
Scene 14:	The following June.

Appendix II

A Postscript on the Major Characters

Sarah Ballenden was unable to make the journey to Fort Vancouver during the two years her husband served there. She spent another lonely winter in Red River, her health slowly deteriorating. She moved to Norway House in the summer of 1852 to live with friends, and travelled from there to Edinburgh with her children in the fall of 1853. She died of consumption in December of that year, just a few months after being reunited with her husband. She was 35.

John Ballenden returned to Red River the summer after Sarah died. His two eldest daughters, Anne and Elizabeth, joined him there later that year. But Ballenden's health had been permanently broken. He resigned in 1855 and returned to Scotland, where he died in December 1856. He was 44.

Christopher Foss travelled from England to Australia in 1852 as officer aboard a convict ship. He was accompanied on the voyage by his wife, four children and a niece. He was court-martialled in Western Australia in 1856 for behaviour unbecoming an officer (essentially, fraud.) He sailed alone to South Australia the following year. He formed a relationship with a woman and had six more children. He died in Bathurst, Australia, in 1890. He was 73.

Adam Thom served as clerk of the court in Red River until 1854, when he returned with his family to Edinburgh. He moved from there to London in 1865 and died there five years later. He was 88.